*To Alan*
*from Noel & Elizabeth*

# GOING FOR IT

*with our love, prayers*
*and sincere best wishes,*

*Noel Davidson*

## NOEL DAVIDSON

*21st L*

**AMBASSADOR INTERNATIONAL**
Greenville, South Carolina • Belfast, Northern Ireland

GOING FOR IT
© Copyright 2007  Noel Davidson

ISBN  978-1-84030-189-2

Ambassador Publications
a division of
Ambassador Productions Ltd.
Providence House
Ardenlee Street,
Belfast,
BT6 8QJ
Northern Ireland
www.ambassador-productions.com

Emerald House
427 Wade Hampton Blvd.
Greenville
SC 29609, USA
www.emeraldhouse.com

# Contents

Introduction ..................................................... 5

## Going for it ... in the fashion
## Amanda's Story

1  This Can't Go On ..................................................... 11
2  Heaven's Gates And Hell's Flames ..................................... 17
3  Under The Apple Tree ................................................ 24
4  Happy Baptism! ...................................................... 30
5  You Have A Degree, You Know! ........................................ 37
6  Motherhood, Management And Ministry ................................. 44

## Going for it ... over the line
## Andrew's Story

1  Is It A Band? ........................................................ 53
2  The Christmas Present ............................................... 58
3  Was Jesus A 'Glen's' Man? ........................................... 62
4  Down On One Knee .................................................... 67
5  Savour The Moment! .................................................. 71
6  Introduce Yourself .................................................. 76

## Going for it ... in a wheelchair
## Craig's Story

1 Mum, Pray! ...................................................85
2 Life For You Will Be What You Make It! ..................90
3 I Want To Push Myself! .....................................94
4 We Will Be Very Pleased To Have You! ..................101
5 First Class ..................................................106
6 Just Like It Used To Be! ..................................113

## Going for it ... in the heat
## Kerri's Story

1 The Big Issue ..............................................121
2 Why Do I Just Want To Cry? ..............................129
3 Shining Out The Other Side ..............................137
4 Teen Challenge ...........................................144
5 What If I Die Here? .......................................151
6 Go For It! .................................................158

## Going for it ... in the net
## Stuart's Story

1 It's OK To Cry You Know, Son ............................171
2 Lovely Young Lady .......................................179
3 What's The World Coming To? ...........................186
4 I'm Starting You Tomorrow ..............................193
5 What Did I Tell You? .....................................200
6 Scoring Goals, Winning Souls ...........................207

# Introduction

SOMETHING IN THE newspaper cutting attracted the publisher's attention. It was about a young Banbridge woman who was one of fifteen volunteers to appear in a BBC TV series to be screened early in 2007. What seemed to fascinate him was a single sentence near the end of the article. This said that she had spent some time studying and working with the Christian organisation, Teen Challenge.

As he and I began discussing the format of a book for this year he said, "I think we ought to find out more about that girl and possibly write her story."

Good idea, but how did we contact her? And did she have a story? If so, would she consider allowing me to write it?

Leading on from that we examined the possibility of finding other young adults from Northern Ireland with interesting and inspiring experiences to share. Could we compile a collection of stories, encompassing a variety of life experiences, but with the central theme of showing the value of a strong Christian faith?

Having set our target I made a few enquiries and contacted Kerri, who came from Banbridge but was now living in London. I hadn't been chatting to her long until I realised that this young lady had led a very active life so far and she sounded so full of zeal for God. When she agreed to talk to me about the prospect of having her experiences included in a book, I recognised that this was my project with the pen for 2007.

After speaking to Kerri I began seeking advice from trusted Christian friends, praying for guidance, and making a list.

Contacts were made and in a marvellous way, and over a period of about six weeks, I had met and spoken to all five of the young adults whose stories I have been delighted to research and recount.

Kerri was my first contact. It was the write-up about her in the 'Belfast Telegraph' that helped develop the concept of this book in our minds. She is an engineer now playing squash on the ladies' professional circuit.

Stuart was happy to be included as soon as I mentioned the idea to him. 'Brother, I would just like everybody to know what God has done for me,' was his reaction. He plays football for Hull City in the English Championship and has 37 caps for Northern Ireland. When not on duty for club or country Stuart spends most of his time working as an assistant to the pastor in his church.

When I talked to Craig about having his story in the book he considered it for a few days before concluding that if I thought his story could help somebody else he would 'be happy to go along with it.' Knowing how he had been left paralysed after a rugby accident at eighteen, yet succeeded in living a profitable life despite daunting odds, I was happy to assure him that his story could be used to help not only 'somebody' but hundreds of people in similar situations. That helped make up his mind and he was in.

Amanda was next of the five to be contacted and I realised after having spoken to her for a short time that she had to be part of the book if she would agree. She had an interesting story of conversion, a pleasant personality, and was branch manager of a leading high-street fashion store. Her husband Mitch was a founder member of Crown Jesus Ministries and she was involved in that work.

The final person to 'come on board' was Andrew, not because he didn't want to, but because he was so busy playing rugby for both Ulster and Ireland that I found him hard to trace. An e-mail one morning brought the reply to my question. 'It sounds like a great idea and I would be very interested in being a part of it,' he wrote. That was exactly the answer I had been praying for. Andrew has 19 international caps for Ireland and is often invited to youth functions to speak about the thrills and challenges of being a Christian sportsman.

What a marvellous mix they have turned out to be, and what an absolute delight to work with. We have talked on the phone and in offices, homes, hotels and restaurants. We have prayed with one another every time we met.

One in a wheelchair.

Two married with families.

Three university graduates.

Four internationals in a variety of sports.

Yet there is a single common and critical factor that unites all five. It is their desire to serve God with all their heart wherever they are. How often over the past nine months have I heard sentiments like, 'I believe this is where God wants me to be,' or, 'Pray for me, Noel. I'm seeking God's will as I move on,' expressed.

It wasn't hard to come up with a title for this book. St. Paul told the Christians in Philippi that he was 'pressing toward the mark for the prize of the high calling of God in Christ Jesus.' 'Pressing toward the mark,' means 'straining forward towards the goal,' or in the language of the up-and-at-it young Christian of today, 'Going for It.'

Writing this book has been a great experience and I would like to thank all the people who have helped me in so many ways as I was rooting about for the information I needed to complete it. These included Amanda's husband, Stuart's wife, Craig's mum, Kerri's friends, Andrew's former housemates and of course my own wife Liz, who is part of everything!

On behalf of Amanda and Andrew, Craig and Kerri, Stuart and myself, and our wider 'supporting cast' I would like to thank you for choosing to read this book. It is our prayer that it will prove a blessing to you. May it lead you to God, or into a closer relationship with Him

Go for it!

**Noel Davidson**
October 2007

# Going for it ...
## in the fashion

# Amanda's
## Story

# 1

# This Can't Go On

"WHY ARE YOU doing this to me?" Amanda Calvert screamed.

She and her school-friend Lynn were at the birthday party of a girl they knew. It was being held in a rugby clubhouse in east Belfast and the two girls had just gone into the toilets. They were followed in by a group of girls one of whom had begun to make snide remarks about Amanda, cheered on by the others.

"What do you mean? I'm not doing anything to you! I'm just telling you what I think of you!" the taunter jeered. Having offered that blunt explanation for her initial spate of verbal abuse she proceeded to follow up it with a second series, designed to be even more offensive.

Lynn and Amanda had been determined to 'have a great night out at this party' and so had begun the evening by drinking enough alcohol to make them tipsy. This they considered an essential prerequisite to 'really enjoying themselves.' Now, with her pride hurt, her mind befuddled and her temper rising Amanda felt she must retaliate.

"Well if you are telling me what you think of me, just let me tell you what I think of you!" she shrieked in retort. Looking her tormentor straight in the eye, and with a voice that continued to rise in pitch, she went on to do that in no uncertain terms.

"Stop it! Stop it!" Lynn shouted at the pair of angry teenagers who seemed ready to come to blows. Fearing that her friend could possibly come off worst if this ugly wordy exchange were to turn 'physical' she dragged Amanda away saying, "Come on, let's get out of here!"

They returned to the main hall where the party was in full swing and Lynn and Dave, Amanda's boyfriend at the time, tried to keep the half-inebriated and totally-incensed girl away from the crowd that she was convinced were 'out to get her.' It didn't work though. Tempers were raised, feelings had been hurt and pride had been dented on both sides and the simmering feud wasn't just going to cool down and disappear.

The chasing clique came after Amanda with a further series of jibes about how she was dressed. It was just too much to take. There could be no holding her now.

Something snapped. Amanda lost control of herself.

Flailing out with hands and feet she waded into the pack leader who fought back fiercely and soon they were in a temper-driven tangle. It was Dave who pulled Amanda away this time and as he endeavoured to hold her in check the enraged protagonists traded insults with each other. When the other girl discovered that Amanda had ripped her 'new shirt' in the melee she was ready to 'go another round,' but was also restrained by some of her friends.

With the two livid young ladies facing each other, but held in check by their respective 'corners,' the feud carried on in the form of a frenzied word-fight. This reached a hysterical pitch and the abuse became even more personal, and embellished with language that Amanda hadn't learnt at Orangefield Presbyterian Sunday School, which she had attended as a child.

Soon everybody was watching. The celebrations had been suspended.

Partygoers had begun to chant and take sides, and what infuriated Amanda was that everybody seemed to be taking the other side. Eventually, when she had become so exhausted and distressed and it was obvious that she was no longer in control of her emotions, Dave said, "Right, Amanda. It's time we were going."

Lynn and he then managed to escort their friend, who was still spitting invective back over her shoulder, out to the cloakroom, then the door and over to Dave's house.

They had some work to do on Amanda before they could take her home. Dave's mum phoned Amanda's with the simple message, "Don't worry about Amanda, Mrs. Calvert. She is with us. I will leave her round in the car later."

Lynn then took on the job of tidying Amanda up, as all the scrabbling at her clothes and pulling of her hair had left her looking nothing at all like the pretty girl who had left home four or five hours earlier. Dave and his mum assumed responsibility for trying to sober her up, plying her with successive cups of coffee.

It took almost an hour, but when Amanda looked more presentable, could walk in a straight line and talk in sensible sentences, then it was time for home. Dave's mum drove Amanda and Lynn, who had arranged to stay overnight with her friend, round to where Amanda lived.

The two girls were barely in through the door until the interrogation started. Amanda's parents had been worried about her daughter's behaviour for some time, but on that particular evening they decided to confront her with a few issues.

"Amanda, who were you with this evening?" mum began.

"You know who I was with," came the instant reply. " I was with Lynn and Dave at a birthday party."

"And have you been drinking?" her dad wanted to know.

"No, I haven't," Amanda tried to assure them.

"Amanda, I think you are lying to us!" Mother voiced a strong suspicion.

"No mum! I am telling you the truth!" her daughter lied.

The argument continued for five or ten minutes until Amanda left the living room in a flurry of frustration, making the excuse that she 'couldn't leave Lynn on her own any longer.'

When she arrived up into the bedroom her friend, who had stuck loyally by her side all evening, enquired, "Amanda, are you in trouble?"

"Not really," came another unconvincing untruth. "It will be O.K. Don't worry."

It wasn't O.K. though. The truth was that Amanda was in trouble.

She couldn't sleep.

Her mind was in a whirl, for her conscience was niggling away at her, and her body felt sick from all the drink she had consumed, despite what she had told her mum and dad.

Amanda spent the remainder of that weekend in physical and mental misery. She had let herself down, Dave down and Lynn down. Why should I end up behaving like that at a friend's party? she asked herself time and again. And the worst thing of all was the deception. She was disgusted at having lied so repeatedly and emphatically to her parents, whom she loved, and who loved her dearly.

When Amanda returned to school on Monday morning her sense of guilt and shame was to lead on to a sense of loneliness and isolation. Lynn was one of a very few of her classmates who even troubled to speak to her. Most of them ignored her completely. Friends of the girl who had invited her to the party the previous Friday night accused her of 'ruining it completely by making a total fool' of herself.

It was so hurtful, so painful.

That was the beginning of a miserable week. Amanda felt so solitary.

'This can't go on,' she kept telling herself, but what was she to do?

Like most girls of her age she was so anxious to feel wanted and appreciated, but she felt the exact opposite, both neglected and despised.

School was a nightmare, for her classmates had begun to shrug her off and freeze her out. Life at home wasn't much better for she had been deceiving her parents for some time. She sensed deep down that her mum knew she was lying all along, but how could she ever confess to all the lies and duplicity?

One night, lying awake in bed, Amanda came to the agonising conclusion that she had become somebody that she didn't like. She would hate to have a friend like Amanda Calvert. So why, then, was it surprising that nobody seemed to like her?

It was a bitter pill to swallow, a hard blow to take.

There was only one way out of this emotional impasse. Amanda decided that for the sake of her sanity and a clear conscience she would have to improve her image, and this would probably mean amending her lifestyle.

How, though, did she go about doing that? It was probably going to be easier said than done, especially attending the same school and into the same class every day.

The situation as it existed wasn't set to last too long, though. It was the summer term and Amanda was soon to sit her GCSE examinations. Once these were over she would be off school for the long vacation. Her aim was to obtain high enough grades in her exams to allow her to embark on the 'A' level programme.

She achieved her goal in this regard and commenced her 'A' level course in September. Amanda had opted to study the sciences and found that only a few of the former classmates who had conspired to make her life a misery for the last two months of the previous term were in her new group. She was very glad of this for it afforded her the opportunity to make a fresh start.

Amanda took one of the first steps in the right direction when she became friendly with Irene. Although the two girls had come up through school at the same time it was not until they found themselves in the Lower Sixth Chemistry class together that they grew to know one another really well. From sitting together in class they began meeting each other during the morning and lunch breaks. Soon they were firm friends and it wasn't long until Irene had introduced Amanda to her twin sister Emily who was also at the school.

This evolving friendship proved to be a tremendous help to Amanda in her endeavour to establish an identity for herself, an identity that would permit her a credible self-esteem. What she liked about Irene and Emily was that they accepted her for who she was, with no strings attached

They didn't criticise what she wore. They had no expectations of how she should perform before being welcomed into their company. They seemed to have no desire to smoke or drink to create or enhance a 'wild and free' image for themselves.

Amanda and Dave weren't 'going out together' any more, but that didn't matter to Irene and Emily. Some of her former friends had used the ability to attract the opposite sex as a yardstick to popularity and acceptance. Not so with the twins.

There was something different about Irene and Emily that appealed to Amanda. They had a sense of peace and contentment about them that she couldn't escape, or indeed at first, explain. The important thing for their mixed-up school-friend was that she felt at ease, and completely safe, with them.

As the autumn term passed and Amanda asked her new friends on Monday mornings what they did at the weekend they would say things like, "Oh yes. It was great. We were out shopping on Saturday afternoon and then went to a Youth conference at night. We were at Bible Class and then church a couple of times as usual on Sunday."

Although Amanda enjoyed Sunday School and Girls Brigade and went to the morning service in Orangefield Presbyterian Church every Sunday, church activities hadn't ever made that kind of an impression on her life. She had been trying to source her 'kicks' elsewhere.

The truth was that Irene and Emily were Christians, and their faith, which they lived out, rather than shouted about, was obviously real to them. Their practical care and companionship helped Amanda to see that it was possible for teenagers to be genuinely happy without having to conform to a certain social code and alienate their parents in the process.

Amanda only saw the twins during schooldays in that autumn term and she still went out with Lynn on a Saturday evening. Although some of the others they were 'hanging around with' considered it 'cool' to spend the time drinking Amanda, made it clear that she wouldn't be having any.

That was when she became aware of someone else who seemed to be happy enough without the booze. Amanda had known Philip, or 'Pip' to his friends, for a long time and he had a friend called Keith Mitchell, whom Pip called 'Mitch.'

Philip was older than Amanda and he often went to something called 'Mannafest' on a Saturday night but afterwards he would make an effort to call in on 'the crowd' wherever they were. He and 'Mitch' would have a Coke each and chat away amicably to everyone. Pip would then make sure everyone 'had a lift home.' Amanda liked Pip, and she had also come to like the look of Mitch, his mate, whom she was soon to discover in another location.

During that first term in Lower Sixth, Amanda's PE group from School went across to the Robinson Leisure Centre nearby for aerobics classes. As Lynn and Amanda were very keen to keep fit for their hockey they often stayed after the other girls had left to work out in the gym.

That was where Amanda came across Mitch again. He was working as a pool attendant in the Centre. Soon she was visiting it more frequently and staying in it longer than necessary, just on the 'off-chance' that she might find an opportune moment to exchange a smile, or better still even a word or two, with Mitch. It wasn't long until she began to sense, and then to hope, that perhaps he was as keen to see her, as she was to see him.

And she was right. Mitch and she were both going to the same church every Sunday morning and she had been looking down on him from the gallery! He sat with his family downstairs and so their paths had never crossed. That, though, was all set to change!

On Sunday February 13, 1994, the day before St. Valentine's Day, Mitch came across to Amanda outside after the service and they began to chat. Before they parted, he had a final question to ask.

It was, "I was wondering, Amanda, if you would like to come out for a meal with me tomorrow night?"

# 2

# Heaven's Gates And Hell's Flames

THERE COULD BE no doubting what Amanda's answer would be. She had been hoping to hear Mitch approach her with a proposal like that for the past three months! It just had to be, "Yes."

The venue for their first 'date' was an Italian restaurant in Belfast's Donegall Pass and it proved to be a most gratifying experience for both of them. Looking into one another's eyes across a well-spread table was a big change from 'eyeing one another up' across a noisy swimming pool or a sombre church service!

Mitch and Amanda discovered that they had common interests since both attended the same church and had differing reasons to be in the same leisure centre, so there was never a lull in conversation. It was a getting-to-hear-all-about-you-and-your- family kind of evening, and since they each felt so comfortable in the other's company they had no problem sharing.

With the meal over the young couple went for a walk around the city centre and then caught a bus up to Mitch's house. Unknown to Amanda he had been planning this night for ages and, since his first night out with her had exceeded all his expectations, he wanted to introduce her to his mum. This meeting also turned out to be a very cordial affair but then it wasn't long until Amanda said, albeit most reluctantly, that she would 'have to go.' Since she was still at school she was obliged 'to be in' before 10.30 p.m. so Mitch's sister-in-law left her home in her car.

Amanda found it hard to get to sleep that night, but for an entirely different reason than some of her earlier insomniac interludes. It wasn't self-examination or self-deprecation that was keeping her awake that night.

On the contrary, it was her self-esteem, which had been given such a whopping boost! The phrase 'the feel-good factor' had taken on a whole new raft of meaning!

That was the start of it. Mitch had met someone he really liked and so had Amanda. The natural progression was that they began seeing each other on a regular basis. Each of them looked forward to every new 'date' with an eagerness that signalled a growing affection.

Amanda had just been 'going out with' Mitch for a little over a month when he found out that there was a dramatic production being staged in the Ulster Temple on the Ravenhill Road in the week leading up to Easter. He suggested that perhaps they could go to it together.

Mitch was a Christian, as were most of his friends, and Amanda admired them for the sense of peace and purpose that surrounded their lives. Going to church was no chore to them and yet they were by no means stuffed shirts or killjoys. She felt the same around Mitch and his mates as she had done with Irene and Emily, respected and secure.

When her new boyfriend had asked her if she would like to come along with him and 'one or two of the other guys' she had no hesitation in accepting the invitation. It didn't matter to her who else was going to be there. If Mitch was going she would be going too, given half a chance!

The play was presented on Wednesday March 30, 1994 and when Mitch, Amanda and their group took their seats in the Ulster Temple they were conscious of people crowding in all around them. By the time the show was due to commence the place was packed. This production, with the strange, indeed almost scary, title of 'Heaven's Gates and Hell's Flames' seemed to have caught the imagination of the people of Belfast.

What struck Amanda from the moment she took her seat was the fact that the stage had been completely covered in silver material. Christian music played softly in the background and the silver stage gave off a dazzling sheen under the lights. She hadn't expected to see the inside of a church done up like this. It made her wonder what was coming next.

Little did she imagine at that moment what a phenomenal impact what was to come next was to have on the rest of her life. After a number of introductory features the main focus of the drama depicted a series of different judgment scenes. These held the entire audience transfixed.

An 'angel' sat centre stage holding a large volume, the title of which had been done in large bold letters so that they were easily visible to the audience. It was 'THE BOOK OF LIFE.'

The first person to come before the angel was a former drug addict who had become a Christian before he died. Having looked through the book the angel smiled, rose and pointed to his right. As the young dishevelled man made his way across the stage in that direction a figure, dressed to represent Jesus, came to welcome him.

A man and woman appeared on stage before the angel after that. They had, according to the story, been killed in a car crash on earth.

"Where are we?!" the woman shrieked. "I never expected to find myself here!"

"I don't know! This is all so sudden and frightening!" the man replied.

Ignoring their conversation, the angel was turning over page after page of the book of life. His face appeared to take on a more concerned look until he eventually closed the book, with a solemn shake of the head. With that he made a solemn sweeping gesture to the left and a personage, dressed to portray the devil, appeared with a couple of demons, to drag them off towards hell's flames.

As they were being pulled away, kicking and screaming the man kept shouting, "There must be some mistake! We have lived good clean lives. My wife is on the catering committee at church and I have been collecting for charities all my life! There has to be some mistake!"

When they disappeared behind the curtain their final screams were bloodcurdling.

Another to appear before the angel was a teenage girl. She had died suddenly and unexpectedly without any medical explanation. The angel checked the book, smiled at her and Jesus welcomed her with the words, "Come in my child."

A different fate awaited the young man killed in a motorbike accident. His cry, in finding himself confronted with an angel bearing The Book Of Life, was, "I can't believe this is happening to me! I went to Sunday School and Bible Class as a boy and up until I was seventeen but I kept putting off coming to Jesus. I thought I had plenty of time! I always intended to become a Christian at some stage, but I was afraid it might cramp my style. I just wanted to enjoy myself for a while!"

The 'devil' and his scurrying little demons got him too.

Amanda was awestruck by all of this but one of the scenes yet to come was to affect her more than all those others by highlighting the ultimate and irreversible tragedy of some of the human issues involved.

A family had been coming home from holiday and the plane had crashed.

They appeared before the angel, and The Book of Life, one by one. The entire scene was enveloped in a sinister silence as the records were scanned. Since only the mother and her son, the youngest of a family of three, could be found there, they were granted admission through heaven's gate.

Father, and the two other children, a boy and a girl, all received the same reaction from the angel. A solemn shake of a bowed and virtually covered head brought the devil and his demons on stage to carry them away. The father's excuse that he was 'a good man but he couldn't see what difference religion had made to the world,' or the daughter's announcement that she 'intended to be saved when she was a bit older,' made no difference whatsoever.

The performance had held Amanda spellbound from beginning to end and it had a profound effect on the seventeen-year-old. It convinced her, in a most graphic manner, of the realities of heaven and hell, and the absolute importance of trusting in Jesus for salvation. In addition to that it also brought home to her that she had no guarantee that she could come to Christ the following week, or even the next day. None of those in the acted-out scenes had expected to appear before the Book of Life judgement as soon as they did, yet the type of events portrayed were happening all around her in the world on a daily basis.

When the play was over an appeal was made. Anyone interested in 'getting right with God by accepting Jesus into their lives' was invited to make their way to the front of the church for counselling. Soft music played and a number of people, some of them in tears, walked slowly towards the front.

Amanda didn't move, though. She knew that this was something she ought to do but she wanted more time to think about it.

When outside afterwards Mitch asked her, "What did you think of that?"

"Aye, it was good," Amanda replied, trying to sound very matter of fact. She went on to change the subject immediately, for she didn't want Mitch to know how she actually felt. Too much talk about it and she would burst out crying. All she wanted to do was get home and be left alone to sort herself out before God.

Mitch sensed what was happening and before leaving her off at home he gave her a booklet called, 'Journey into Life' and a book, 'It Makes Sense,' by Stephen Gougrodger. "You might like to have a look at these, Amanda," he suggested.

Later that evening in the bedroom which she shared with her sister, Amanda lay in bed and read all the pamphlets that Mitch had given her. She switched out the light and lay staring into the silent darkness of her bedroom. Her sister was already asleep in the other bed.

Within minutes she was out of bed and sitting in the middle of the floor in the dark. Her mind was in turmoil. She knew what she must do. Moving over to kneel beside her bed she prayed that God would forgive her sins, and then asked Jesus to come into her heart and life, believing that He had died for her and was calling her to come.

As she knelt there, elbows on the bed, head cupped in her hands, Amanda felt a sense of tranquillity take over in her mind, driving out the turmoil of ten minutes before. She then climbed back into bed, and after a short time spent basking in a glow of contentment, drifted off to sleep.

Mitch wasn't working the next day and Amanda and he went to Dublin for a trip in the train. Amanda knew that she must tell him what had happened the previous evening. She wanted him to be the first to know, and was sure he would be delighted. When was she going to get the chance, or find the words, to tell him, though? That was her problem.

Walking along O'Connell Street she wanted to break the good news to him, but found she couldn't. Sitting in Bewley's café chatting over a cup of coffee would have been the ideal spot to bring up the subject, but again she couldn't.

Realising that time was fast running out on her she determined to tell him on the train on the way home. She must find some way to let him know before they arrived back in Belfast.

The train was packed. Every seat was taken.

Mitch and Amanda had taken seats at a window facing each other across a table in the hope of being on their own. With the crowd that just seemed to keep piling into the carriage there was no hope of that happening, however. A man and woman were soon occupying the seats beside them.

Was Amanda going to hold back again? She was longing to put Mitch in the picture but circumstances weren't making it any easier!

It was when they were about halfway between Dublin and Belfast and the Enterprise was hurtling along at full speed that the conversation turned to a tack that allowed Amanda to share her brilliant news.

They had been discussing the train and the speed it was doing when Amanda remarked, "Wouldn't it be awful if this thing were to crash?"

"You are right it would," her boyfriend replied. "There would be absolute carnage if it did. Lots of people would be killed."

He paused for a moment, and possibly influenced by the previous evening's performance went on to add quietly, "At least I know where I'm going if anything like that should ever happen to me."

Looking across at him, and making sure she had caught his eye, Amanda responded softly, "So do I."

"What do you mean?" Mitch asked, surprised and delighted. He would love to believe what he was hearing, but just had to be sure that he had heard it right.

"I mean that I'm a Christian too," Amanda went on to explain, relieved that she had been able to witness to her newly found faith at last. "I asked Jesus to come into my life after I went in last night."

Mitch was thrilled and almost overcome with emotion. He half stood up to reach forward wanting to take Amanda in his arms and hug her with joy. He thought better of it, though, and slowly sat down again, his eyes filling with tears. It would be wonderful to dance up and down the aisle shouting 'Praise the Lord!' but he was forced to settle for taking both her hands in his and exclaiming, "That's great! That's great!"

It had been a good day out together up until that moment but then the needle on the happiness register shot up so high that it nearly went off the scale. There was so much to talk about, for not only were Mitch and Amanda revelling in a maturing love for one another, but they were now also united in their Christian faith.

In the days immediately following Amanda's conversion Mitch commenced an especially tailored 'counselling course for new Christians' with her. This was conducted with genuine loving care!

Towards the end of the Easter holiday from school Amanda and Mitch were invited to a party and two of those also attending were another pair with whom

Amanda had wanted to share her life-transforming experience. They were Irene and Emily.

Having assumed that she would have to wait until the commencement of the summer term before being able to speak to them in person, Amanda was glad to learn that they were expected to be at the party. She had no inhibitions about letting these girls know that she had come to Jesus!

As soon as she spotted the twins at the opposite side of the room that evening she made a beeline across to them.

"I have something to tell you!" were her opening words.

"What is it?" both girls seemed to ask at once, but Amanda had the sneaking feeling that she was about to tell them something they already knew.

Reaching down to pull the end of a necklace she was wearing out from below her top, Amanda held, in the palm of her hand, the cross that was on the chain. Her mum had given her the necklace as a present a year or two previously, but she had a completely new reason for wearing it now. The cross had taken on a very personal significance for her in the past week!

Irene and Emily looked at the cross she was holding up to them and as they did so Amanda clarified what she meant so that the situation could be understood beyond any reasonable doubt. "I have become a Christian!" she told them, her face beaming.

"That's terrific!" one replied, while the other had a telling observation to make.

"We were almost certain that something wonderful like that had happened from the moment we saw you come into the room," she said.

"What made you think that?" Amanda wanted to know.

"Well look at you! You are just radiant!" Emily explained. "I have never seen you look so happy in my life." With that she proceeded to give her friend a warm hug.

"We just knew that you would come to Jesus," Irene went on. "You see we have both been praying for you!"

"O thank you!" Amanda cried and put an arm around each of them.

Another set of friendships, which had been constructed with mutual care, was now cemented with Christian love.

# 3

# Under The Apple Tree

ALTHOUGH MITCH AND the twins were overjoyed at Amanda's conversion, her mum had reservations about it. Her daughter hadn't told her about what had happened on the Wednesday night before Easter, but Mum Calvert had noticed a definite change in Amanda's style of life. This was most evident in her choice of reading material and in the places she seemed keen to go to with Mitch.

A Bible, a book of daily readings and some other items of Christian literature had replaced the pile of teenage-girl type magazines on her bedside table. Now, too, she seemed to have developed an insatiable appetite for attending 'religious' meetings all over the city. Mitch had a lot of Christian friends in different churches across Belfast and enjoyed visiting them for their Sunday services. He found the more charismatic type of service more in line with his spiritual fervour than the more traditional forms, but Amanda didn't really care about such things at that stage. Anywhere Mitch went she was more than happy to go too!

Mrs. Calvert found 'this business of going to other places' hard to fathom. It had always been her policy to support the Sunday services in her 'own church.' She had brought the family along with her, as well as sending them to all the children's and youth activities in the church, expecting that they would probably follow her example. It was hard then to see why Amanda needed to be running to all these 'other denominations' some of them even in 'wee halls.'

When Amanda sensed from a couple of comments her mum had made on different occasions, out of genuine concern, that she feared her daughter was possibly doing the right thing for the wrong reason, or possibly evening the wrong way, she recognised that it was time to clear up the issue.

"I just want to tell you. Mum," she said, "that I am reading my Bible because I really like to, and going to other churches with Mitch because I really want to. I'm not doing these things just to please Mitch. One night before Easter this year I became a Christian, and I am now enjoying living for Jesus."

Mum was probably only about seventy-five per cent convinced by this declaration, but as time went on she discovered that it was true. There could be no doubting that Amanda was a very pleasant and helpful daughter around the house. Perhaps her motives, and the experiences she claimed to have with God, were genuine after all.

Despite her mum's unease at her going to other churches with Mitch, Amanda found the exposure to different types of service and forms of worship an enlightening experience. She was pleased to attend Orangefield Presbyterian Church and loved meeting the committed Christians there, but it was also thrilling to find out that there were others in the city, in a variety of churches and fellowships, who loved the Lord with exactly the same fervour as herself. Coming from a traditional Presbyterian background she found some of the forms of worship 'very different,' but it was clear nonetheless that these people were both earnest in their faith and energetic in their approach to evangelism.

No matter where Mitch went on a Sunday evening he always made an effort to be back, if at all possible, to Orangefield for the Sunday Night Youth Fellowship. Although Amanda relished the opportunity to 'see how it was done' elsewhere she also liked to be back for SNYF. She enjoyed being with others of her own age from the church, and she also learnt a lot about living the Christian life from those responsible for the Bible teaching from week to week.

As summer approached, Amanda was busy studying for her end-of-year Lower Sixth examinations during the week but was always out with Mitch at the weekend, and she seldom missed SNYF on a Sunday. When it came time for the Sunday Night Youth Fellowship to close down for the summer Mitch and Pip were very concerned.

They were worried because the upper age limit for SNYF was 18 and this meant that two guys who had been coming every Sunday night throughout their teenage years were going to be excluded in September. As neither of them had as yet made a Christian commitment the friends considered it unacceptable that the church should expect them to go somewhere else, and possibly end up going nowhere, on a Sunday evening.

Pip, Mitch and Amanda discussed the situation often and each of them prayed that God would guide them in the path they felt convinced was His will for them, and for those who had become too old for SNYF. They decided to approach the minister and the church elders with their vision of starting a group for anyone of 18+ in the church hall on a Sunday evening, at the same time as the Youth Fellowship.

There were a number of meetings over the summer months with the church leaders. Since they were always anxious to encourage any group which showed an interest in extending its influence in, and outreach to, its own members and the local community, they gave the idea their whole-hearted support.

A committee of six was selected to establish this new venture in the autumn. Appreciating that gatherings such as they were planning to initiate usually benefited from having an appropriately descriptive name, one of their first jobs was to set about choosing one. A further period of prayerful discussion took place on this subject and eventually it was agreed that their meeting or fellowship or whatever it was going to be, should be called 'Access.' This was selected as the best of all those suggested, and favoured because of the verses from Romans chapter five in the Bible, which had inspired it initially. These assure the Christian that 'having been justified by faith, we have peace with God through our Lord Jesus Christ, through whom we have access by faith into this grace in which we stand, and rejoice in hope of the glory of God.'

During her Upper Sixth year that followed Amanda was happily engrossed in her studies in school during the week and her commitments in church at the weekends. It was the year of the two 'A's, Access and 'A' levels.

The committee had put a lot of thought, work and prayer into planning an autumn programme for Access, but on the opening night in September only the six of them plus one other guy turned up. The team were only slightly disappointed at this for the chap who did come was one of those they had been concerned about losing. And it picked up from there. More came the following week and even more the week after that.

It was a big challenge for the leadership team, for up until then none of them had any experience in organising that kind of a group, but God blessed their efforts nonetheless. Never having done it before meant that they approached the task with an enthusiastic spiritual freshness and Access began to attract many young adults from other churches to Orangefield Presbyterian after the normal services on a Sunday evening.

As a member of the committee, Amanda had to speak occasionally at the weekly meetings and to do this effectively she had to engage in some in-depth Bible study. Although she had only been a Christian for less than six months Amanda had hit the spiritual ground running!

In the early summer months of 1995 Amanda became gradually aware of a creeping uncertainty that occasionally threatened to cloud the happiness on her immediate horizon. It was the realisation that her 'A' level results would be coming out in August.

She had applied to study Physiotherapy at the Ulster University in Jordanstown but during the weeks prior to sitting her examinations in early June had begun to feel deep down that she wasn't going to obtain the required grades. Life was good all around her. Amanda was going out with Mitch, learning eagerly about her Christian faith and excited to be involved in different aspects of church work with her friends. These were all thrilling things to be doing. Sitting in for hours at a time on warm summer evenings revising Maths or Chemistry didn't hold quite the same appeal somehow.

Her niggling premonition proved to be well founded. When her results came through on the appointed date she had achieved good grades by many standards but they did not meet the entrance requirements for her Physiotherapy course.

Amanda was devastated.

In spite of her frequent misgivings, she had always hoped that some kind of a miracle would occur, and she would obtain the grades she needed. This hadn't happened.

The totally distraught teenager couldn't bear to be with anybody, not to mention discuss the matter with them, that morning. All Amanda wanted was to be left alone. Having shut herself off in her bedroom for most of the morning she resorted to lying out in the back garden under an apple tree in the afternoon. It was a sunny day and she eventually cried herself to sleep in the sympathetic shadow of the tree.

Nothing seemed to matter any more now. Her dream of becoming a physiotherapist had been smashed into smithereens by a few capital letters on a small, official-looking piece of paper.

Some time later the comforting bliss of sleep was interrupted by a familiar voice saying softly, "Amanda. Wakey – wakey! It's me,"

Struggling to open her tear-reddened eyes and look out into the bright sunlight Amanda saw a figure standing a couple of metres away in the garden, as though not quite sure whether to wake her up or not. If anyone could bring her any kind of comfort it would be this one person. Mitch.

Amanda burst into tears again. Having barely spoken to anybody about her deep disappointment all day she began to pour out her heart to her boyfriend. "I don't understand this, Mitch," she said. "The only thing I want to do is study Physiotherapy. And now I can't. Why has God allowed this to happen to me?"

Mitch listened patiently to what she had to say, interrupting only occasionally to make sympathetic comments like, "Yes, I know," or "I understand." When Amanda had completed her litany of self-pity and had sat quietly reflective for a few moments Mitch thought that he had better address the spiritual implications of the issue. He knew it wasn't the time for a treatise on 'all things working together for good,' but what he did say was most significant.

"Maybe God has other plans for you, Amanda," he suggested.

It was a consoling concept and one that became more meaningful when Amanda received a letter from the Admissions Branch of the Ulster University a few days later informing her that they were prepared to offer her a place on a degree course studying Applied Biochemical Science. The big incentive in this was that the letter stated if she attained a certain standard set by the University in the first-year course she could switch to studying Physiotherapy in her second year.

Amanda was learning a lesson. It was simply that although she was now a Christian everything wasn't going to work out exactly as she had wanted it to or imagined it would.

Soon after starting her studies at UUJ in October Amanda became friendly with a fellow-student in the same position as herself. This girl had also been informed that if she were to finish in the top five in her year-group she could transfer to the Physiotherapy course.

They encouraged and helped each other from the beginning as both were determined to achieve a common goal. This paid off, and by the middle of the academic year Amanda and her friend were both well up in the course rankings and on target to make the required grades in the final results in May.

At that stage, however, a peculiar thing happened.

Amanda began to realise that she had lost the hunger for physiotherapy. She was enjoying her current Biological Science course and felt that it was what she should have been doing all along. It didn't cause her a lot of heart-searching to determine that, regardless of her results in the end of year exams, she wouldn't be changing course.

Perhaps Mitch had been right.

Maybe God had other plans for Amanda.

# 4

# Happy Baptism!

AS AMANDA'S COURSE incorporated the award of a Diploma in Industrial Studies the Ulster University arranged for her, along with another girl from the group, to spend her third year 'out,' at the Esso Research Centre outside Oxford in England. She began her work at the Centre in October 1997 and found herself sharing a house in the village of Wantage with two other students.

She approached the prospect of her year in Esso with a mixture of excitement and trepidation. It was going to be thrilling to work with a huge multinational company. How, though, was she going to cope without the emotional support of Mitch and her own family and the spiritual stability of Mitch and her friends in Access? Could she establish and maintain a Christian witness alone, and depending solely on God?

Her work in Esso involved research into the performance of oil in engines and Amanda loved every minute of it. She found working as part of a team designing and running various tests and then analysing the results an interesting experience.

The social and spiritual aspects of living out of the comfortable cocoon of her home life cycle caused her concern, however. Recognising that one of her priorities ought to be to find a lively church in which to worship, Amanda began to make a few enquiries. Having been delighted to discover that her male housemate was a Christian she asked his advice and he recommended a Pentecostal-type community church, which met in the village school.

Amanda began to attend the services in this fellowship and was made most welcome. With being so close to a famous university city the church leaders in the Wantage fellowship were used to having students visit them, and the young woman from Northern Ireland soon felt at home as she began going there.

She found the lifestyle of the Christians she encountered in England to be quite different to what she was used to at home, however. It was not uncommon for them to meet for a social drink in a pub after a service. Amanda found this strange when invited to join them, and with her background of teenage binge drinking, a huge temptation.

Although she began by having only soft drinks it wasn't long until she thought that seeing these people who were all Christians were having a glass of wine 'there couldn't be any harm in it.' There may not have been for them, either, but what Amanda hadn't realised about herself was that she couldn't control her appetite for alcohol, once she began, quite innocently, to drink again.

The year progressed, and with money in her purse the persistent problem of always wanting to feel 'accepted' plaguing her mind, she found herself, indulging more than was advisable. This worried Amanda. When she came, next day, to read her Bible and try to commune with God in her quiet time, she would dissolve into tears and pray for forgiveness. She felt that she had let God, Mitch. Access, the workmates amongst whom she should have been witnessing, and not least herself, down.

"I'll never do it again," she pledged before God.

But perhaps a fortnight or three weeks later she had broken her vow and was at it again. And she felt gutted again.

The first half of the year turned out to be a real spiritual roller coaster. She enjoyed the worship in the community church and felt very close to God during the services. When Amanda was on her own, though, she struggled to find complete contentment in her soul, because she felt that she wasn't living a consistent Christian life.

With all the spiritual props from home stripped away Amanda began to realise, subconsciously at first, and then with a slowly dawning awareness, that God was teaching her a vital lesson. It was simply that she was a Christian because she had a personal and unique relationship with Him. She was accountable to God, and to Him alone, for all her actions.

Her Heavenly Father had dropped his struggling child, Amanda Calvert, in the heart of England to allow her to, quite literally, 'work out her own salvation with fear and trembling.' No other person, however spiritual or sympathetic, or church body, however welcoming or wise, could do that for her.

As Easter 1998 approached, Amanda gradually became more settled in both mind and spirit. She began to draw her strength from God, asking Him to help her make the proper decisions, even if they were not image-enhancing 'popular' decisions.

A trip home to Belfast over the Easter holiday period turned out to be a time of spiritual and emotional renewal. Amanda saw Mitch and their friends from the church again, and heard some thrilling family news.

About a month before she had been due to come home Amanda phoned her younger sister, Fiona, whose birthday was coming up just before the holiday. She wanted to know if there was anything in particular she would like as a present.

There was a momentary silence on the line and then Fiona said softly, "Could you get me a Bible?"

"Of course I could!" Amanda replied, delighted. "Is there any particular reason why you would like a Bible?"

"No, not really," little sister replied. "I just thought I would like a nice Bible."

That was fine by Amanda, but when she handed over the carefully selected gift she had bought the first time she saw Fiona after arriving home, the truth came out.

Having told Amanda how much she loved her birthday present, Fiona went on to add, "I knew you were the best person to ask to get me a Bible. You see I became a Christian a couple of months ago."

"That's wonderful news!" big sister exclaimed. "I have been praying for you and all the rest of the family since I gave my own life to the Lord. But why did you not tell me when I was on the phone?"

"I didn't feel I was ready to. I just wanted to be sure in my own mind that it was real, or something. It's hard to explain," was Fiona's somewhat bumbling response.

Amanda had no option but to reassure her, "Yes, OK, I know what you mean." Although thrilled at her sister's confession of faith she couldn't remonstrate much more about the delay before she had been told about it. After all she hadn't been exactly running around witnessing to everybody after her own conversion!

There was intense political activity up in Stormont Castle, a short distance from her home, that Easter weekend. The 'Good Friday Agreement' was being negotiated and then signed and was, despite some tension and dissention, hailed as a forerunner to lasting peace in Northern Ireland.

When she returned to England to finish out her year with Esso, Amanda hoped that it would achieve its aim, but whatever happened in her native province she had been refreshed by having constantly recalled the original 'Good Friday Agreement.' Under the terms of that settlement people could have peace in their hearts and feel reconciled to God because of Jesus' death on the cross. She had also been enveloped by a sense of peace and privilege, which in turn provoked an outpouring of praise, when she remembered that it had been just before Good Friday, four years before, that she had committed her life to Christ.

On Sunday morning, May 17, the church pastor came across to where Amanda was sitting and said, "Would you like to lead us in prayer for Northern Ireland this morning? Perhaps you could explain a bit about this referendum that is taking place next Friday, and the prospects for peace in the country before you pray." Then, stopping to nod towards a man sitting on the other side of the hall, he went on to add, "That guy over there is from Northern Ireland as well and he is going to share too."

As she was coming in Amanda had noticed the pastor speaking to a man she had never seen before. On hearing that he was from Northern Ireland Amanda made a mental note to have a word with him after the service and find out why he was visiting their village.

Having agreed to do as the pastor had suggested Amanda felt very nervous. She had been following the political events back at home very closely and with her city often being headline news she sometimes felt awfully homesick. How she would have loved to be in the buzz of it. Now, though, she was being offered the opportunity to explain briefly the implications of what was happening in the province, and lead the congregation in prayer.

She prayed passionately and silently that God would help her to focus on the right things as she spoke during, and pray intelligently publicly at the end of, her review.

The 'guy over there' spoke first and then prayed in an unmistakeable Northern Irish accent, before Amanda, who was standing at the front beside him, took over. She began by mentioning the trauma of 'the Troubles' before going on to express the heartfelt hope of everyone for peace and reconciliation, of the lasting variety that only God could provide, in the country.

It was when she started to pray, however, that a depth of passion, at which she was surprised herself, became evident. Words came tumbling out of her mouth without her even thinking them. Amanda became very emotional and tears streamed down her cheeks as she felt a deep sense of God's compassion for the situation 'back home.' She felt that her breaking heart was merely a human extension of His divine heart of love.

When Amanda had finished interceding with such obvious conviction the pastor then continued to pray for peace in Northern Ireland. It was during this prayer that Amanda dared open her eyes when she heard a sound of shuffling. Some people were turning around in their seats to slip down on to their knees. Many of the congregation were crying.

After the service a number of people came up to Amanda and thanked her for her contribution to the service that morning, describing it variously as 'most moving' and 'a revelation from God.' There could be no doubt about it. She knew it in her soul. God had used her to help these people understand what was happening in Northern Ireland and hopefully they would now be able to intercede for the province in a more meaningful way.

Having spoken to all those who had come over to see her, Amanda suddenly remembered the 'guy over there.' When she went looking for him he was nowhere to be found! She caught up with the pastor who was busy preparing to close up and asked him, "That man from Northern Ireland. Who is he? Where is he from? Where is he staying?"

The pastor looked just a little embarrassed to be replying, "I'm sorry but the answer to all your questions is, 'I don't know.' He sounded genuine enough when he came in and said he would like to ask for prayer for Northern Ireland. I thought it was a good idea, and then felt I ought to ask you as well. It was amazing the way in which he opened up the subject for you. Thanks Amanda."

The whole episode was indeed, as the pastor had described it, 'amazing.' On reflecting upon it on her way home and for days afterwards Amanda found that it had helped restore a sense of purpose to her life. It was as though God was saying. 'I have a purpose for your life, Amanda. I have given you, and shown you how to use, the specific gift of prayer and intercession for others.'

Inspired by this confidence Amanda decided that if God were going to use her in His service she would have to be more courageous in her witness for Him to those around her. The ideal opportunity to make a public confession of her faith came when the pastor announced one Sunday morning that they were 'going to be holding a baptismal service in two weeks.' This announcement came with an invitation to anyone wishing to openly confess the Lord in baptism by immersion. They were to 'speak to me at the end of the service.'

Amanda took him up on his invitation and went asking to be baptised. The pastor was more than happy to include her on the list for the baptismal service and Amanda began praying for the grace and courage to ask all her house- and most of her work-mates along. She had phoned Mitch to tell him and he was pleased that she was prepared to take this step of openly confessing her faith, but unfortunately he wouldn't be able to be present.

When the morning of the baptism came Amanda was chuffed to discover that most of the friends she had invited had actually turned up. Knowing that she would be expected to say how she had come to faith in Christ and why she wanted to be baptised as part of the service, Amanda took the opportunity to set the record straight before God and with her contemporaries. "I have to say sorry to some people present, and also to God for how I behaved when I first came over here. I feel I have let you, God and myself down in this, " she confessed, before continuing with, "Please forgive me. I am using my baptism service as a public pledge that I will be endeavouring to live for God before you, as best I can in the future."

With that she was baptised and felt a tremendous sense of the peace of God, which defies human description, flood her soul. This had been the right thing to do. As well as being in obedience to the command of God it had constituted an ideal opportunity to make a public stand for Him.

As Amanda was leaving the church a couple of the girls came across to her and one of them said, obviously speaking for both, "What you have done and said today has really touched us. We admire your courage and would like to know more about your faith. Thanks Amanda."

What Amanda didn't realise, though, was that while these friends were talking to her a number of the others had gone on back to the house to prepare a barbecue in her honour. She was moved by this gesture and when they produced a huge chocolate cake with the words 'Happy Baptism' scrolled across it in white icing, the tears welled up in her eyes. Although her friends may not have appreciated the deeply spiritual significance of her baptism they knew that it meant a lot to Amanda and were prepared to celebrate it with her in the way they considered most appropriate.

God had taught her lesson number two. Her year in England would soon be coming to an end and He had shown her in this, her last month, that her honest Christian testimony, however shaky at the start, had been respected by those amongst whom she had been living and working. The message was that if she shone as a light for God, wherever she happened to be, people would be attracted to Him.

# 5

# You Have A Degree,
# You Know!

SOON AFTER COMPLETING her 'year out' in England, Amanda was off again. This was during the summer of 1998 when she went on a mission trip to Kenya with Access. Eleven young adults from the group based in Orangefield Presbyterian Church had given up two weeks of their summer vacation to go out to the African country to engage in outreach work with Loresho Community Church, which is affiliated to the Presbyterian Church of East Africa. The pastor from Loresho had spent a two-year term on secondment in Orangefield and it was on his invitation that the visit was arranged.

Coming, as it did, not long after her intercessory experience in the Wantage church, and then her baptism, this trip allowed Amanda to appreciate even more fully the hand of God on her life. The team made many valuable contacts through a series of different outreach strategies and saw a number of young people come to faith in Christ.

It was in the home where she was staying, however, that she witnessed the most telling manifestation of the power of God to change lives through simple witness.

A lovely couple from the Kenyan church had indicated that they were prepared to offer accommodation to three of the visiting group and Amanda was sharing their home with Fiona and Roger. As the trio began to feel at ease with their very caring host and hostess it seemed the most natural thing in the world, when they arrived home in the evening after what could have been a physically exhausting but nonetheless spiritually rewarding day, to share their experiences with them. Both the man and the lady of the house seemed so interested in all that was going on, constantly asking questions and offering encouragement.

Amanda found it so easy to be herself, and share all the ups and downs of each day with these most hospitable people. She was ideally suited to the role with her easy, friendly nature, an expansive vocabulary, and above all a bubbling enthusiasm for Christian outreach.

It was not until the group was preparing to leave Africa to return to Northern Ireland that the three housemates were to learn the profound effect these evening sharing sessions were having on their hostess. They had been talking openly about their faith, about how great God was, about the marvellous things He had done in their lives and what He was currently doing on this mission trip. Amanda and her companions had all assumed that this man and woman were both Christians, for after all who but Christians would be happy to have a bunch of Bible-buffs like them in their home? And listen to them babbling on about contacts and commitments, preaching and praying, salvation and dedication, every night?

What a surprise, and shock, they were to receive then, the night before they left when the lady, who had been so kind to them for almost a fortnight, said she had 'something to tell' them. It was simply that she hadn't in fact, been a Christian when they came into her home. Their love for Jesus, and others for His sake, had been so obvious, though, that it was almost infectious and spoke to her heart. The thrilling 'something' she had to tell them was that the previous evening, as a result of their consistent witness, she had asked Jesus into her life!

Amanda arrived back in Belfast to commence her final year in University with a renewed zeal for God and interest in Christian service. Being back at home, however, after having been away for some time was to test her Christian patience from time to time. Having lived in England for more than a year, when she could come and go as she pleased, she began to find her parents' understandable concern for her, reflected in their questions when she was going out in the evenings, a little irksome.

Whether it was Mitch she was going out with, or some of her church or university friends, it made no difference. It always seemed to be the same. It could be either, 'Who are you seeing this evening, Amanda?' or, 'Where are you going?' or 'When will you be home?'

The answer when given, was usually accompanied by the thought, which was very occasionally translated into a comment, spoken hopefully like a Christian in control, "I'm twenty-one now, you know!"

This growing sense of Amanda wanting to establish a personal identity for herself intensified at the end of that summer when Mitch and she began to have serious discussions about their future. Mitch had always maintained that God had brought them together, and that Amanda was the woman with whom he was meant to share his life.

Amanda agreed that he was right, for she felt the same about him. Before they made any lasting pledges to one another though, she felt that she ought to be honest with him about her shaky start to the year in England. Although long since behind her it was on her conscience and she had to come clean about it. This was important as well because she knew that Mitch was interested in becoming involved in full-time Christian ministry.

Was Mitch sure that she could measure up as his wife in that context? She had no wish to be an impediment in his life, an obstacle to his ardour.

As a pair of sincere and honest Christians in love with each other Mitch and Amanda had a number of discussions about these matters. Both were perfectly candid on everything from what would happen if Mitch felt he ought to leave his job in the Fire Service to become an evangelist to what would happen if Amanda were to get a job with a biochemical company 'somewhere else.'

The process of talking about the prospects for the future were all done with a consciousness of the importance of seeking the will of God for their lives, and when they continued to do this Amanda and Mitch were both totally convinced they were meant to marry. On Saturday November 28, 1998, they went out for a meal together in the Old Schoolhouse, Killinchy, Mitch proposed to Amanda and they announced their engagement.

Amanda's final year at university was very busy and yet she settled to her studies with a strong determination. With a ring on her finger, marriage on her mind and God and Mitch in her heart, she was intent on doing well and securing 'a good job.' Her application to study paid off, for Amanda graduated with Second Class Honours, First Division, in Applied Biochemical Science.

During the summer that followed Amanda lost the interest in obtaining employment that had helped to motivate her during her final year at university. A sense of anticlimax took over in her mind. It were as though she felt that now she had a good degree God was going to arrange for someone to come knocking on her door some day and say, "Excuse me, are you Amanda Calvert? If you are, we have a job for you. Would you like to come and work for a high salary in our world famous biochemical company? Just sign there at the bottom of the page."

It didn't work out that way.

Summer cooled down into autumn and still Amanda had no job. Mitch and her dad kept saying, "Amanda, you will have to get out there and start looking. In case you didn't know, jobs don't just land in your lap!"

Wanting to be seen to be taking their advice Amanda started looking in the Situations Vacant sections of the local and national newspapers. But she was very fussy. She knew what she wanted. There were jobs available for people with degrees in biochemistry, but they were mostly working in labs, and Amanda didn't want to work in a lab. Sitting in her white coat, on her own, carrying out successive tests and analysing endless results didn't appeal to her as a fulfilling way to spend the remainder of her life.

Amanda wanted to work in sales. She wanted to work with people, selling something to somebody. Two sales jobs in the biochemical industry did come up and Amanda applied for them, full of hope. Could either of these be the opening she was waiting for?

She didn't get either of them for she 'didn't have any experience.' This was the age-old question, asked by hundreds of young, and often well qualified people. 'I can't get a job because I have no experience, and yet how am I to gain experience if I can't get a job?!' It was frustrating.

There were times when she was tempted to ask, just as she had done after her 'A' level results, 'What's going on here, God? I was thoroughly convinced that You led me into my degree course, and now I can't find suitable work.'

After a fruitless autumn on the jobs front Amanda took up a part-time sales post in the Oasis fashion store in Donegall Place in Belfast city centre. Although she was only working 20 hours a week at first Amanda enjoyed the buzz of meeting people and she loved selling. She was pleased to be offered full-time hours over the Christmas period but kept telling herself, 'This is only a temporary measure. I have a degree and something better will turn up in the New Year.'

The prospect of 'something better' did 'turn up in the New Year,' too.

Amanda saw advertised, and applied for, a post as a sales representative with a major chemical company, covering the whole of Ireland. It was just what she wanted and after an initial interview was invited, along with one other girl, to a final interview in England.

This went really well, or so Amanda thought. She answered all that was asked of her and felt the interviewing panel was satisfied with her performance. They told her before she left that the successful applicant would be notified by telephone within the next two days.

That sounded reasonable enough. There was nothing left for Amanda to do now but go home and wait for the call.

But it didn't come.

After the third day came and there was still no news Amanda thought that they must surely have lost her phone number. She would just give them a ring to remind them. It wasn't a good move, though, for that was when she learnt the gut-wrenching news. 'Sorry, Amanda, but the post has already been filled.'

This was unbelievable. Amanda just couldn't take it in. She had come home convinced that the post was hers and had already begun to sort out in her mind how she was going to tackle it.

On making further enquiries as to why she had been unsuccessful Amanda was informed that the panel found that there was little or no difference between the other girl and herself. They were both considered excellent candidates. The deciding factor had been that the other applicant had 'experience,' and Amanda didn't.

Oh, no! she thought. Not again!

This really was a devastating blow to an ambitious young woman.

She had thought that this must be the job God had for her, but it took her many days and much prayer to convince herself that it must not have been.

There was always Oasis, though. Amanda had carried on working there even after Christmas and when a full-time post became vacant in the shop she applied for it and was appointed. This was a boost to her confidence but it seemed to sound alarm bells in the minds of the two men she most loved, her fiancé and her father.

"That's good, Amanda," each of them said at different times, before going on to add, "But you have a degree, you know! You should be earning twice, maybe even three times as much as you will be getting in Oasis!"

Amanda knew that. She didn't need to be told it every week. Had she not applied for jobs in keeping with her qualifications, but been unsuccessful for she lacked 'experience?' Mitch and Dad couldn't help noticing, despite their expressed concerns, that with every week that passed Amanda appeared to be growing to relish the customer contact and challenge of selling in the city centre fashion chain even more.

In the summer of 1999 a vacancy arose for a supervisor in the Oasis concession in Debenham's. Amanda was eager to develop her skills and so approached her manager asking if she could be trained to an appropriate level to allow her to apply for the post

Her boss told her that she had the potential to make a good manager, with her degree, experience, and track-record in selling. At last she had that elusive, and apparently critical criterion, 'experience!' The store manager was prepared to train Amanda, but on one condition. She would be required to commit to them for at least a year. Amanda accepted this, but it left her with a problem.

Could she do that? What if she saw another lucrative sales post with a chemical company advertised next month? How would she feel?

It was 'make your mind up time.'

Amanda asked for time to consider the matter and as she prayed about it became convinced that this was what God had been planning for her all along. She would have the opportunity to live for Him amongst people every day, manage staff and stock, and sell stuff. And if she ended up selling clothes instead of chemicals what did it matter? Was it not all selling in the long run?

During that busy summer in which Amanda was undergoing management training with Oasis she was also preparing for what was to be one of the most important events in her life. Mitch and she had set their wedding date. They were to be 'united in holy matrimony' on Friday, October 20, 2000.

On completing her training and applying for the position Amanda was told that she would be transferred to a supervisor's post in the Oasis concession in Debenham's, in one of Belfast's busiest shopping malls, Castle Court, as from November 1.

This she saw as a divine provision. At last it all seemed to be coming together. God was unfolding His plan. Mitch and she would be married in October and she would have a new job opportunity waiting on her return from honeymoon.

Mitch and Amanda were determined that their wedding in Orangefield Presbyterian Church, in addition to seeing two loving hearts united in one, should also serve as both a celebration of, and a witness to, the importance of their Christian faith.

The young couple had told the minister that they would like him, in whatever way he considered most appropriate, to present the Gospel message. Mitch and Amanda backed this up by asking him to make it clear that the newly-weds had left something for every guest in the pews. It was a copy of the booklet 'Journey Into Life.'

Above all they were anxious to let it be known, both in the ceremony and at the reception, that their wedding represented not merely a two-fold, but a three-fold fusion. It was not a line but a triangle. It was a public declaration of an eternal union between Mitch, Amanda and God.

That was the testimony of their wedding day, and that was how they vowed to spend the rest of their lives. God was to be their pilot, provider, protector and final court of appeal, in everything.

# 6

# Motherhood, Management
# And Ministry

LIFE AS A NEW wife was so exciting!

Amanda arrived home from honeymoon to a triple challenge. She was establishing a new home, starting work in a different store, and anxious to support Mitch in every possible way in his passion for seeing others brought to Christ.

The commissioning service for Crown Jesus Ministries, as Mitch and two friends had decided to call the Christian ministry they had established in east Belfast, was held in Orangefield Presbyterian Church at the end of November. As Amanda sat listening while her husband, Philip Kerr and Stephen Thompson were commissioned as evangelists she felt a warm glow of satisfaction. The church minister and Stephen's pastor from Beersbridge Road Elim Church both gave solemn and stirring addresses of commission and Amanda felt privileged to be part of it. She had just married one of these committed young men and was thrilled to have done so. It was another milestone reached along the road on her journey with God.

She took to the home-making easily and working in the new store presented few problems. Clothes were clothes and if customers knew what they wanted Amanda could sell them something. And if they didn't know what they wanted it was her job to make her displays so attractive that they knew what they wanted before long and had it paid for, and in an Oasis bag before they walked away.

Keen, not only to help her husband in his ministry but also to develop her own personal spiritual contribution to their combined witness, Amanda prayed that God would show her an individual and effective role that she could undertake for Him. She would be happy for this to be with Crown Jesus Ministries or something else completely different, as long as it helped see either people brought to know the Lord or Christians strengthened in their faith, or both.

It wasn't long before God revealed to her what an important back-up ministry she was to organise. The work of Crown Jesus Ministries had taken off and was still soaring. God was blessing the work of Pip, Stephen and Mitch across Belfast and they were beginning to be invited to organise Gospel outreach events amongst young and old in other parts of the province. The expansion of this work meant that the three evangelists were encountering an ever-increasing variety of physical and spiritual needs among the people they met in their ministry. This in turn, gave rise to a growing opportunity to pray for, and occasionally with, seeking and hurting people.

That was where Amanda came in. Having heard Mitch and the others articulate this need more than once she discussed it with him and agreed to organise a ministry of prayer and intercession. She had never forgotten how God had blessed when she prayed in that service in Wantage more than two years before. She had felt then that perhaps this was a 'gifting from God' that she could use to help advance His kingdom. It was now her turn to pray for guidance as to how best to tackle this most important challenge.

There were a number of prayer topics which it would not be considered prudent to share publicly. These included personal requests for prayer that the members of the Ministries team were receiving, and some of the difficulties they were encountering, as they engaged in different aspects of their work. Amanda started another group to pray earnestly and particularly for such matters. This was a small cell of discreet and dedicated Christians who could be contacted at short notice and were referred to as the Intercessors.

Not long after assuming responsibility for the prayer ministry team Amanda attended a course on the importance of prayer, organised by Rev. Derek McKelvey. This focussed on different aspects of prayer ministry and drew its examples from the Bible. She found it extremely helpful and was soon encouraged by how God was using her to pray specifically for people during ministry times.

As Amanda's self-confidence grew through an increasing number of speaking engagements in church situations so she began to transfer this belief in her ability to communicate with and inspire others, to the workplace. Here it wasn't the passion for seeing Christian women, including herself, fired up to intercede with God more effectively that motivated her. It was rather the enthusiastic desire to see all those who worked with her reach their full potential both personally and in their work.

In April 2001, just five months after starting in the new location, Amanda was promoted from supervisor to assistant manager in the Oasis shop in Debenham's. Two years later the post of manager in the same store became vacant and Amanda applied for it and was appointed.

This senior position allowed her to put into practice what she learnt both from her training and experience, and sales under her leadership were good.

Amanda loved the buzz of her life in those days. She was taking ever more meetings on the theme of prayer and intercession as well as speaking at evangelistic events with 'the boys' from Crown Jesus Ministries. She also enjoyed the challenge of managing both staff and stock and pushing sales figures in her store even higher.

When she had been almost two years managing the Oasis store in Debenham's, the company advertised two jobs simultaneously. The first of these was the post of manager in its store in the Forestside shopping complex, which was close to where Mitch and Amanda lived, and the other was for a Development Manager.

Both of these jobs appealed to Amanda, so she applied for the two of them. She would have been happy to accept either, but was delighted to be selected for both! The interviewing panel for the job of Development Officer had obviously been aware of her passion for encouraging her staff to achieve their full personal and sales potential.

Before formally accepting this job Amanda felt that she ought to share a piece of news that had thrilled Mitch and her, but which her employers might not find quite so gratifying.

Amanda was expecting her first baby!

Her bosses were quite happy to take her on, they said, provided her pregnancy wouldn't restrict her ability to travel, as the Development Manager would be required to make frequent trips to London. Amanda said that it shouldn't and neither it did. She made 12 return flights to London between taking up the position and stopping work to have the baby, and suffered no ill effects.

In May 2005 Amanda began working as manager in the Oasis shop in Forestside. This presented yet another series of challenges. She had to acquaint herself with the system in a different store, the personalities and potential of a different staff, and the buying preferences of a different clientele. Amanda loved that kind of testing situation. She had long since learnt 'to be herself, and try to see every day as an opportunity to reach into other people's lives for Jesus, so a change of position or personnel usually failed to faze her.

As the summer months approached Amanda had other appointments to keep. These were in antenatal clinics and classes and as the privileges and responsibilities of parenthood slowly unfolded in their minds Mitch and she began to pray and plan for their unborn baby. It had such a bonding effect as they shared joyfully their aspirations for their son or daughter to be.

There was just one niggling concern that worried Amanda. She had always been convinced that God had led her into helping organise the vital prayer and intercession element in Crown Jesus Ministries. Was the joy of being a devoted mother going to curtail her activities in this regard? Could she possibly juggle meetings and motherhood?

This question was answered for her one evening towards the end of the Hillsborough Bible Week in July when many people, including the parents-to-be, had remained behind for a prayer and dedication session after the evening meeting. Amanda was standing up to pray with Mitch sitting beside her, leaning forward. Placing one hand on her husband's shoulder and the other on her bump, the Intercessors coordinator brought her own very special request to God. "Lord, bless my family," she prayed earnestly, inwardly. "Help me to be a good wife and mother. I know that fulfilling these functions to the best of my ability is also an important part of my ministry for You."

As she stood there, moved with emotion, God seemed to reassure her that it was most important to be a good wife and mother, and carrying out these callings with diligence and Christian love would enhance rather than hinder her ministry.

Mitch and Amanda were proud to welcome baby Noah into their lives, hearts and home on October 3, 2005. Amanda had expected life to be different with a little son to look after, and she had been absolutely right.

She needn't have worried about whether or not she could continue her involvement with Crown Jesus Ministries. It was such a thrill to nurse her baby boy, and then watch all the stages of development as he grew month by month that she almost begrudged the time spent doing anything else. When Mitch, who was keen to see her get back into the spiritual 'swing of things,' offered to baby-sit to allow her to go out to a meeting of some sort, she had to push herself to do so.

Amanda's first major speaking engagement after Noah's birth came when he was nearly six months old. Crown Jesus Ministries were conducting a partner church outreach project in the city of Lisburn in the spring of 2006 and Amanda was invited to share in the service in the Kingdom Life Church on Sunday, March 26.

Anxious to be her best for God she prepared thoroughly for this meeting and a few days before she was due to take it Mitch happened to enquire quite casually, "What are you speaking about on Sunday, Amanda?"

"On the work of the Holy Spirit, I think," his wife said.

"I don't think that's what they are looking for," Mitch replied, looking rather surprised. "Did you not remember that Sunday is Mother's Day? That's probably why they asked you to speak in that service. What with being a new mother and all."

"Oh, yes, I see what you mean," Amanda had to admit. "I'll have to get to work on something else."

She did, and when she gave an address on Mary the mother of Jesus it was well received, with some of the congregation claiming to have been 'particularly blessed' by it.

This was her first time back before an audience since Noah was born and a few days later, at the beginning of April, she was due to clock-up another 'first.' It was to be her first day back at work since taking off to start her family. Mitch hadn't been all that keen for her to return to work but when he asked, "Do you really have to go back, Amanda?" he had to agree that his wife had a point when she replied, "Well, if I don't go back into Oasis we will have to move out of here."

Their situation was not uncommon among couples in their twenties. Both of them needed to work to pay a mortgage and maintain a reasonable standard of living.

During her time off having Noah Amanda had informed the senior management of Oasis that she would come back to manage the store in Forestside but that she would be relinquishing the job of Development Officer. The store in the shopping centre was less than a mile from her home, but frequent trips to London were completely out of the question now.

Amanda did some of her weekly shopping in Forestside and when she called into the Oasis store to show off her new baby the sole question the staff had to ask was, "Amanda, when are you coming back? We miss you!"

Much to their pleasure she returned as arranged and it was to prove a challenging time, just getting things 'back into her way of going' again. The shop had a good summer of trading, however, and by the autumn things had been turned around. With work back on track Amanda was soon to be faced with a different question in relation to her involvement with Crown Jesus Ministries.

The imaginative Christian organisation was arranging a One Way youth weekend in the Ulster Temple during October. They were anxious to know if she would be interested in taking part in this. Would she do something with the girls, for instance?

Rather than giving an answer right away, Amanda asked for time to think it over. She knew that it would mean a lot of work, but here was a chance to become actively involved again in the work that had always been the joy of her heart, seeing young people reached for Jesus. Was she ready for it, though? She was loving motherhood and enjoying management. Was this the time to add ministry to the mix once more?

Having prayed about it and talked it over with Mitch and some of the others at Crown Jesus Ministries Amanda finally decided that this was the time. Yes. She would arrange a fashion show for the girls on the Saturday afternoon. When she met the committee organising the weekend she agreed to speak at one of the morning seminars as well.

On hearing the subject she was to speak about she almost changed her mind. 'Being a Princess for God.' The idea of the girls' meetings was to highlight roles that young Christian women could play in life. There were three subjects for the talks, Princess, Daughter and Warrior.

It sounded ever so 'cheesy' at first, but when Amanda began to look into the Bible and think of the privileges that came with being the daughter of a King, she quite warmed to the subject. She could make something of it after all.

The fashion show would test Amanda's organisational skills to the limit. Not only had she planned to draw from her own store in Forestside but most of the other fashion outlets in the complex had also agreed to participate. It was a lot of work but it would be worth it. Amanda had to put all thoughts of the afternoon fashion show on hold during the morning, though. She was to be the first speaker in the opening seminar.

Everyone listened intently as she spoke from personal experience about what it meant to be a 'Princess' waiting for her 'Prince.' Many hearts were touched. It had been so worthwhile. Amanda felt at home.

As the next speaker took to the stage she was barely listening. She was struck by a sudden realisation.

This was the Ulster Temple. This was the building in which she had determined to give her life to Christ. Now here she was again, lost in reflection, twelve and a half years later. So much had happened during that time. As Amanda looked back she saw how all the strangely-shaped pieces had fitted into place in God's jigsaw puzzle of her life, to make the complete picture.

A lump came in her throat and a tear in her eye.

She was back in ministry.

And that is how she plans in the will, and with the help of, God, for it to continue. She wants to mother her family, manage her store, and minister to others, all for His glory.

# Going for it ...
## over the line

# Andrew's
## Story

# 1

# Is It A Band?

"JOHN THREE AND sixteen states it very clearly," Matthew Wright told the teenage lads.

He and his brother had been taking a stroll along Portstewart promenade on a sunny summer afternoon when they met some boys coming laughing and larking along and had stopped to talk to them. They recognised each other from church connections and Matthew was trying to direct the conversation away from insignificant, and round towards important, issues.

"John three and sixteen. What's that?" young Andrew Trimble asked.

"Don't tell me you don't know what John three and sixteen is!" Matthew continued, rather astonished.

"Is it a band?" Craig Knight, one of Andrew's mates, enquired in all seriousness.

Everybody laughed, but as he talked on Matthew realized that although they thought Craig's question a huge joke, the truth was that not a single one of these lads had a clue about John three and sixteen. It could just as easily have been a band as anything else as far as they were concerned. They hadn't a notion.

"It's a verse from the Bible," Matthew informed the group, who appeared surprisingly interested. He went on to quote it to them and explain what it meant as concisely as possible.

This apparent lack of any kind of background Bible knowledge among these young people concerned Matthew. Others also felt strongly that something ought to be done to teach teenagers like these the basic truths of the Christian faith. Some of them had been going along to Exodus in Coleraine on Saturday nights. The Exodus focus, however, was on giving somewhat older and already at least slightly clued-up Christian young people somewhere to meet socially, and not basic or intensive Bible study.

When fifteen-year-old Andrew Trimble heard that 'Matt' as he called him, plus 'Stevie' Moore and Diane Rossborough, were planning to start a Bible study in Matt's house in Portrush he was very happy. Craig, Timmy Higgins and some of his other friends had also been asked to go along and were as pleased at the prospect as he was.

Perhaps going to something like this would allow him to come up with answers to some of the questions that had begun to pop up now and again in his mind. There seemed to be a great cloud of uncertainty hanging over him. And out of that cloud there came three distinct questions. One of these concerned himself, a second was about his future, and a third was in relation to some of the guys he had met at school.

'Who am I, and what am I here for?' he would wonder from time to time. 'Is there any purpose to life or is it just a case of be born, grow up, go to school, get a job and eventually grow old and die?'

His concerns about the future were two-fold. 'What is going to happen to me when I leave school and try to make something of myself in life?' he would worry. Then there was the whole question of death and what happened after it. Was there, for instance, 'a big beyond,' and if there was, where was it, or how could anybody know anything about it?

Andrew lived with his parents and two older sisters in Coleraine and attended the town's Academical Institution. When he was in third form there two of his friends, Paul Campbell and Neil Morrison, invited him to go with them to a few meetings of the Christian Union in the school.

He agreed to go without any reservations and Andrew was amazed at a couple of things he found there. The initial surprise came when he discovered how enthusiastically the guys at the 'CU' talked about the Bible. He thought this a bit strange. Big strong lads, many of whom were older than him, and people he looked up to because of their strength and skill on the rugby field, waxing lyrical about Jesus. Why would they want to do this? he would like to know.

This gave rise to a second query and it was not so easily defined, nor was there, as far as he could see, an easy tick-box answer to it. It was to do with these guys and their whole attitude and personal demeanour. They all seemed so satisfied with life, as if they had something to live for and were in control of their own destiny. None of them appeared to have the hang-ups he had about personal identity and purpose or fear of the future.

The vital question was, what did they have that he hadn't? What was their big secret?

The Bible studies in Matt's house were to provide answers to most of these questions. The young people who gathered on that first Saturday evening weren't quite sure what to expect. They knew that they were going for a light meal and then a period of 'Bible study' whatever that meant.

Matt, Stevie and Diane had prepared thoroughly for the event, providing food for the body and then a Bible for anyone who didn't have one. This was the 'plate' from which they hoped to serve up stimulus to the mind and challenge to the soul.

After the meal was over and the table had been cleared the Bibles appeared on it and Matt took charge. He wanted, he said, to study with them the subject of 'What is the Gospel?'

The leaders had to help some of their 'students' find 1 Corinthians chapter 15 in the book before them, as Matt said he wanted to focus his study on the first few verses of that chapter. That would be a good place to begin, he suggested, for it contained a very concise description of 'The gospel.'

That was where Paul, the man who had written the book, declared that he had preached the gospel. This was 'that Christ died for our sins according to the Scriptures, and that he was buried, and that He rose again the third day according to the Scriptures.'

Matt then began to explain about the death of Christ for our sins, and about His burial and resurrection. He allowed time for questions and discussion as they went along and before anyone knew it an hour had passed! When it was time to pack up and head off to Exodus Matt and the other leaders were a bit worried that it had gone on too long. Maybe it had all been too much for 'the kids' to take in at one giant bite. Perhaps they would never want to come back.

They needn't have worried. Andrew and his mates weren't thinking that way at all. As the leaders were driving them across to Exodus in their cars and heard adjectives like 'great' and 'fabulous' and 'amazing' used to describe the time they had spent learning about 'the gospel,' it was their turn to be astonished.

That was the beginning of a series of Bible studies that gave a group of keen young people a basic understanding of fundamental Christian beliefs as well as addressing some of the questions they asked or were likely to be asked. Topics such as 'How can I know that God exists?' or 'How can I be sure that the Bible is true?' created an active interest and launched some lively discussions among the roomful of teenagers.

One evening, after they had spent nearly two hours considering Isaiah chapter 53, and how it foretold the sufferings of Christ, Andrew and a number of the others remarked to the leaders, "We didn't know that there was anything about Jesus in the Old Testament. Why have we never heard this in church?"

It wasn't all noses in the Bibles stuff either, and that was another of the things that Andrew liked about 'hanging out' with this 'crowd.' If the weather was good on the afternoon or evening they were meeting the leaders were quite liable to suggest that they 'go round to Dunluce Castle and do some cliff-jumping.'

Some of the group were already Christians, and others like Andrew at the beginning, weren't. The mix didn't matter, and as Andrew studied the Word of God in depth with the group, he also began to read it personally alone, at home. As he did so he realised that the peace the Christian people he knew, both at the School CU, and in 'Matt's Bible Study group' as he called it, had in their lives, stemmed from having a living faith in Christ.

This was what he was lacking, he concluded, and he determined to do something about it. On a Saturday night in November 2001, when he had just turned seventeen, in Exodus in Coleraine, Andrew Trimble bowed his head at a table and asked Jesus to come into his heart and life. There was nothing dramatic about it. It was just a simple commitment of himself to the Lord, a sincere response to Christ's call to 'Come to Me,' accompanied by an inner pledge and determination to live for Him.

Thus began a completely new phase in Andrew's life. The Bible studies that had once meant so much to him became even more meaningful then, and the relationship with his Christian friends much more rewarding.

There were other developments taking place in Andrew's life around that time too. The sports coaches at school had recognised his outstanding talent on the rugby field from the day he first turned out to practice as a first-former and by fifth year he had become an established member of the Coleraine Inst. 2 nd XV.

When he moved on into Lower VI he began playing for the 1 st XV and was selected to attend a trial for Ulster Schools. Andrew looked on this as a great honour and it was while he was looking forward to his first trial that he had a text from Matt Wright who had received it from someone else and been challenged by it.

Andrew read it over and over again on his mobile. It was so gripping for it forced him to put his present life and possible future career into perspective.

It said, 'Life is a coin. You can spend it any way you like but you can only spend it once. Don't pursue money, power, pleasure or fame, for one day you will meet a Man who cares for none of these things, and you will realise how rich you really are.'

The young Christian saved that message. It could prove a useful motto for him in days to come. It would certainly help him keep his feet firmly planted on the ground and his life priorities in the proper order. Especially if 'money, power, pleasure or fame' should ever come his way.

# 2

# The Christmas Present

ON JULY 11, 2002 the Coleraine Inst. Rugby 1st XV went on a tour of South Africa. This was a great experience for Andrew in a number of ways. To start with there was the excitement of foreign travel and the challenge of playing rugby against lads of his own age in a different country and culture. It was against this often-formidable opposition that his outstanding ability as a player became evident.

The biggest thrill of all, though, was the unfolding revelation that dedicated Christians could be dedicated rugby players. This came when he realised that some of the guys who were with him in the team on the tour, selected because they were amongst the best in the school at the sport, were also unashamed Christians.

This was the practical answer to the enigma of his first visit to the school CU. How could some guys who seemed to me made of steel on the pitch suddenly go all soft and sentimental at the thought of Jesus?

Now Andrew understood just how they felt. He knew what moved and motivated them. He had become one of them.

Ben Steen, another lad who had become a Christian during Matt's Bible studies and whom Andrew had come to know much better through them, was also on tour. Andrew, Ben and two of the other members of the touring team met up at regular intervals, to pray and read the Bible together. They always made sure, too, that they met briefly for a time of prayer before each match. These committed young guys were constantly conscious that they belonged to a different kingdom and served a higher Master and considered bringing everything to Him in prayer a privilege and a pleasure. It was a natural reaction rather than an ominous chore.

The informality of the tour allowed Andrew and Ben to share their faith with some of the other lads in most congenial circumstances. They went on safari as part of their trip and sitting around the campfire, in the stillness of an African night Andrew and Ben seized every opportunity that came their way to talk about what it meant to be a Christian.

Andrew Trimble began his Upper Sixth year as Head Boy of Coleraine Academical Institution, captain of the 1 st XV and a member of the Ulster Schools Rugby squad. On the first Saturday in October he proved his rapidly developing prowess as a player by scoring an outstanding try for his school team against old rivals Royal Belfast Academical Institution. Andrew picked up the ball deep in his own half and ran strongly for three-quarters of the length of the pitch to score at the other end. The young flier was beginning to show his class!

Later that month he scored his first try for Ulster Schools in a match against Lancashire Schools at Deramore Park, Belfast. Soon after this he was notified that he had been selected to represent Ireland at schoolboy level and would be playing for his country later in the year.

It was all happening for Andrew. In the space of a term he had reached further peaks in his career. He was playing rugby for C.A.I. in the Northern Ireland Schools' Cup competition and Ulster. Now he had been chosen to play for Ireland. His outstanding speed and skill in the three-quarter line had been recognised by the selectors. This naturally modest young man off the field was a strong tackler on it. He had also the ability to run at and through the opposing defences and score tries. Andrew was the kind of player every school coach dreams of having on his team.

Later that year Andrew received a most unusual, but very much appreciated Christmas present. Unknown to him, his dad had won a photograph of David Humphreys in his Ireland shirt, at a raffle in the local rugby club. David was at that time commanding a regular place in the Ireland team and scoring a lot of points for them with his goal-kicking and was one of Andrew's 'heroes.' He even afforded himself the luxury of dreaming sometimes of being another player from Ulster to follow David into a full Ireland shirt. When he was younger it had all seemed 'pie in the sky' but had his selection for Ireland Schools brought it any closer?

Dad knew of his son's admiration for the Irish out-half and this gave him an idea of what to do with the photo. He made a few enquiries, which led him to interesting contacts, and when Christmas came around he had a unique present for his son.

Andrew tore off the wrapping to reveal a framed photograph of David with a personal message inscribed on it. This read. 'Congratulations on being selected for Ulster and Irish Schools' and was signed 'David Humphreys.'

This immediately took pride of place amongst the growing collection of rugby memorabilia in his bedroom. It was a treasured possession. 'Will I ever be as good as David?' the eighteen-year old wondered as he looked at it.

He hadn't long to ponder this question, however, for later in the Christmas holidays he was out in pursuit of that aim. His first match for Ireland Schoolboys was against the Ireland Under-19 team at University College Dublin in late December. Andrew marked his debut for his country by scoring a try.

There were other games at School and for Ulster before Andrew next turned out in an Ireland shirt against the schoolboy teams from France, England and Wales over the Easter vacation 2003. The Irish team, with Andrew playing in the centre, won all three matches. His best performance of the series was in the match against England at St. Mary's Rugby Club, Dublin. That was when he exploded down the field, jinking and swerving, and although the opposition tried valiantly to stop him, those who managed to touch him couldn't hold him. Andrew was in for another try.

It was peculiar but as the opposition became tougher and the standard of rugby stepped up a level, Andrew just seemed to raise his game to keep pace with the change. And it all seemed so effortless! Others who had played on the Ulster Schools team with him hadn't made it to the Irish squad. He had, and he was showing fantastic bursts of speed and touches of flair. Looked like there was more to come!

When the rugby season was almost finished and Andrew had started to study for A-level examinations rather than train for powering runs down the wing, he was awarded the first personal achievement trophy of his rugby career. He was invited along to the Awards night of Ulster Rugby on Thursday 15 May 2003, and presented with the Schools Player of the Year Award.

Having completed his A-levels Andrew Trimble left school in June 2003 but he didn't leave off playing rugby. He continued to train with the Irish Rugby Academy in Belfast over the summer, and although he was still only eighteen years old he was approached by Ballymena Rugby Club and asked if he would consider playing senior level rugby with them the following season. Andrew agreed to their proposal and committed himself to the County Antrim Club for a year at least.

Everything was coming together at once. Was he going to be able to make a career in rugby? Was he ever going to be as good as the man whose photograph he looked at every night in his bedroom?

Despite the fact that he was beginning to be acknowledged as an up-and-coming unmistakeable talent by rugby commentators Andrew was very aware that he also wanted to grow in his Christian faith and live his life in a manner that would be pleasing to God.

He would love to be able to prove to all with whom he came in contact that people who can appear fired up with physical determination when on a rugby pitch can display the care and compassion of Christ, both on and off it.

# 3

# Was Jesus A 'Glen's' Man?

WHEN HIS A-LEVEL results came out in August 2003 Andrew was offered a place in Queen's University, Belfast, to study physics. He was still involved in playing rugby for Ulster and when training with the Ulster under-21's he met Stephen Auld, who was already a student at Queen's.

Stephen had heard about this new guy, Andrew Trimble, who was coming to join the Under-21 squad. When he learnt from his contacts that Andrew was a Christian he felt he would like to encourage him.

This led him to approach the new player the first day they were together in the dressing room.

"Hi Andrew," he said. "Welcome to the squad. I'm Steve Auld. Somebody told me you are a Christian and I just wanted you to know I am too. I will be glad to help you if there is anything I can do."

Andrew was pleased Steve had made himself known. He only knew some of these players, and to find that one of those he hadn't met before was a Christian was a reassuring bonus.

What Andrew didn't know at the time, though, was that Steve was just about to start his second year at Queen's and he had a house in South Belfast with two vacant rooms in it. The lads who had been in them had moved out and Steve was on the lookout for new housemates.

When Andrew heard about this from some of the other guys on the team it was then his turn to seek out Steve. At a later training session he asked him about the vacant rooms and Steve told him that one of them had already been taken but he would be welcome to the other. He suggested that Andrew come round to Lower Windsor Avenue sometime to have a look at it, and when he did they agreed Andrew would move in at the start of the university term.

With the question of accommodation sorted out Andrew could concentrate on preparing for the start of his university career. He did this, not by embarking on a programme of pre-term study but by doing what he did best, playing rugby. He had started training with and playing for Ballymena and he was also continuing to work out with the Irish Rugby Academy in Belfast.

In September, before moving to Belfast, Andrew was invited to talk to a group of teenagers in the Boys Brigade in Rathfriland, Co. Down. Mark Scott, a Christian lad who played beside Andrew in the centre for Ulster and Ireland Schools, was a leader in that BB Company and invited Andrew along.

The boys enjoyed a series of video clips Mark had compiled of Andrew and him playing together on the same team in different matches. They also had a good laugh when Mark made fun of Andrew for not scoring when it seemed he had an obvious opportunity.

Mark's idea in inviting Andrew to come to the BB that night, though, wasn't that they should spend the whole evening talking about rugby, although most of the lads had a keen interest in sport. He wanted them to hear about Andrew's Christian faith, and how it influenced his life, both on and off the pitch.

They sat totally engrossed as Andrew was interviewed in relation to a number of issues involved in being a Christian sportsman. The evening concluded with a question and answer session, with the boys having more questions than Andrew had time to answer.

This was the first time Andrew had been asked to share his faith in a public meeting. Never having done anything like that before he hadn't been quite sure what to expect, but the rugby reference at the beginning had made an easy introduction and he believed it had been worthwhile. He hoped he had succeeded in getting across the discovery he had made when still at school. Dedicated sportsmen can be dedicated Christians.

When Andrew first began training with Ballymena Rugby Football Club he showed the same passion and dedication for his new club as he had displayed for all the school teams he had represented. He wanted to be the best he could be, for God, who had given him his exceptional talent.

He had only played a few matches for Ballymena as an eighteen-year-old, not long out of school, when the team coach was heard to remark, "That young fellow Andrew Trimble is going to go all the way."

As though to prove him right Andrew showed just how important a player he could be for his new club in a memorable match away to Galwegians on Saturday November1. Ballymena had travelled south and west to Galway for the match and were coming under a lot of pressure in the opening quarter of the game. That was when Andrew scored two breakaway tries in quick succession to turn the tide. He had come bursting through the centre to leave the opposition standing and add valuable points to the scoreboard in what ended up in a 30 points to 6 win for the visitors.

Moving in to rent a room in Steve's house was to prove a tremendous spiritual blessing to Andrew. Steve had been a leader in Portadown Christian Endeavour before coming up to Queen's but he hadn't left his zeal for Christian outreach behind him in the County Armagh town. He was a student at the Belfast university but his overriding passion was to see young Christians meeting for Bible study and prayer and as many people as possible confronted with the challenge of committing their lives to Jesus

Andrew hadn't been long in the house until he had identified Steve's motto for living. It was a Bible verse that he quoted often. Steve was constantly echoing the words of Jesus in John chapter 10, when He declared, 'I have come that they may have life; and have it to the full.'

Fired up by Steve's unremitting enthusiasm the other three lads sharing his house learnt how to live life to the full. And as a result of their passion for sharing their faith with others, their house in Lower Windsor Avenue was usually full as well!

Andrew had to travel to Ballymena on Tuesday and Thursday evenings for rugby training but Monday and Wednesday evenings were Bible Study evenings. A number of their friends attended the Christian Union in Queen's on a Monday evening but they invariably ended up with Steve and Andrew and the others in the house, with their Bibles open, discussing some point or other.

Wednesday evening was more structured. Steve had begun having regular Bible studies for anyone from Portadown CE who was now either studying or working in 'the city.' When others heard about these studies they asked if they could come too and no genuine would-be Bible student was ever turned away! These meetings had a time when they were supposed to start but no time was set on when they were supposed to finish. The Bible study was over when the last person who didn't happen to be sleeping there that night left the house, and that was often in the 'wee small hours of the morning.'

Living life to the full for the four lads in the house meant having lots of fun. Their Christianity wasn't a dead religion. The natural competitive edge they all possessed meant they were constantly inventing new games and challenges for themselves. The TV in the house didn't work but that didn't matter. They didn't need it.

Visiting friends could be invited to take part in impromptu games of indoor cricket, or house climbs where the competitor had to move from the hall to the top floor of the house without allowing his of her feet to touch the floor.

Steve and Andrew also enjoyed arranging darts competitions with a difference. 'Darts in the dark,' or 'darks' as the boys called them, were played on winter evenings with the room lights off. This could be a challenging activity and resulted in some peculiar scores! One of the residents was a keen photographer and he produced a 'horror movie' in the house over a couple of weeks.

These guys, who enjoyed playing improvised games with, and all kinds of tricks on each other, had a very serious outlook in regard to their Christian responsibilities. They wanted the people they worked and studied with, and lived beside, to understand why they were so happy in, and with, life.

In addition to the house Bible studies, which were open to anybody who felt like dropping in, there was the attempt to reach out with the good news of new life in Christ to the people round about. Andrew often joined Steve in going door-to-door on their street and in the surrounding streets. They would spend an evening telling people about Jesus and inviting them along to the studies in Lower Windsor Avenue.

Perhaps one of the most effective methods they used for transmitting the Christian message to those in the street was the Bible verses they used to put up in the windows. Many people passed their house, particularly at the weekends going to football matches in nearby Windsor Park, and Steve, Andrew and friends saw this as an opportunity to present them with a challenge from the Bible.

Theirs was an end house with large windows at the front and side, so this allowed the lads to print out texts in as large letters as they could possibly fit on to the sheet of paper that filled the window. The end window looked out on a funeral director's premises further down the street, so the message it carried for many weeks was, 'For the wages of sin is death, but the gift of God is eternal life in Christ Jesus our Lord. Romans 6: 23.'

Bold statements such as 'There is no difference, for all have sinned and fall short of the glory of God. Romans 3: 23' or 'The fool has said in his heart, There is no God. Psalm 14: 1,' gave rise to all kinds of enquiries from people passing. Some of these were students who, seeing any of the lads about the door would ask something like, 'What does that mean, to 'fall short of the glory of God? ' or, ' Are you trying to say atheists are fools?'

Friday and Saturday nights particularly brought a number of drunks onto the street and some of them would even bang on the door, and then ask whoever came to it, what 'all this stuff' meant.

It was the banner announcing, 'Jesus said, I am the Way, the Truth and the Life. John 14: 6' that brought a peculiar enquiry from an intoxicated supporter of the Belfast football team, Glentoran, late one evening.

Andrew and a couple of his friends were approaching the house and the man, who had been standing unsteadily looking at the poster was just starting to move away. Seeing the three about to go into the house he shouted at them, "Was Jesus a Glen's man?"

That was a hard one. The only answer the inebriated enquirer would be likely to understand was, "No I don't think He was. But He wants you to come and join His team. He has paid the transfer fee. All You have to do is go to Him and sign up!"

# 4

# Down On One Knee

AT THE START of the 2004-05 university year Andrew switched courses at Queen's University, opting to study Theology rather that Physics. There were no switches in his rugby career, however. It just continued to move forward steadily.

Since he had become a regular in the Ulster Under 21 squad, Andrew did his training with them and the Irish Rugby Academy during the week, and played his club rugby with Ballymena at the weekends. It was a busy schedule but with Andrew's tireless enthusiasm it was easily manageable.

Life had now become more structured. It was study at University, rugby training during the week with a game on Saturday, and the continuing interest in the often late-night Bible studies with Steve and friends.

During that year Andrew played in all five Ulster under-21 matches. The first of these was a friendly away to Gloucester, followed by the inter-provincials against Leinster, Munster and Connacht. Their most encouraging match of the season, though, was against New Zealand Youth.

This team was on a tour of Canada, Britain and Ireland and were unbeaten in all the games they had played until they met the Ulster under-21s at Ravenhill,

Belfast, on Saturday, November 20, 2004. Ulster dominated this encounter and ended up defeating the touring team by 34 points to 13.

In April 2005 Andrew signed a development contract with Ulster. This was yet another step up the rugby ladder, coming, as it did at the same time as he was involved in playing for Ireland Under-21s in the Six Nations competition.

As the season progressed Andrew had played some great games for Ballymena, and had been singled out as Man of the Match a number of times. Now he was hoping to show that kind of quality in an Ireland shirt.

The series of matches began well enough with an away win in Italy but then started to go downhill with defeats against Scotland and England.

Andrew was a keen competitor and he didn't like to beaten. He was also a keen Christian and wanted to show the rest of the young men on the team that this meant something to him. How could he demonstrate that his Christianity wasn't just a Sunday morning added-extra, but an essential ingredient of his life?

He decided to ask the other guys on the team if it would be OK if he prayed with them before the start of the next match. This was at home to France and although Andrew went to the game determined to pray before they took the field as a team, when it came to that point he didn't seem to be able to find the courage to do it. He chickened out at the last minute.

Afterwards, when Ireland had lost 13 – 30 to the visitors Andrew felt frustrated. An inexplicable fear of something, whether of ridicule or embarrassment he couldn't be quite sure, had held him back from fulfilling what had been a definite intention.

It wasn't that he imagined praying before the game started would have made any difference to the final score. As a team player he was obviously disappointed by the result, but that wasn't his only reason for regret. This stemmed from a sense of personal failure. He felt he had let God down, and somehow failed in his relationship with Him. The only consolation was that he had one more chance to come. The final match of the competition was away to Wales and he was totally determined to pray with the boys on the team before it.

Would he, though, or would be back off again?

This fixture was to be played at the Ospreys rugby ground and it was Andrew's last opportunity of the season to carry out his resolve. He must seize it.

Before the team left the dressing room Andrew asked them, as he found them in groups of three or four, if they minded if he prayed with them as a team before kick-off. The Ulster players on the Irish team knew about Andrew's strong Christian faith, but most from the other provinces probably didn't, at least until that moment. They were possibly a little surprised at the prospect of prayer on the pitch, but no one expressed any objections.

That approach helped prepare the way and at the end of the pre-match warm-up all the players gathered around Andrew on the pitch. He dropped down on to one knee on the Welsh turf and prayed briefly for God's blessing on them as a team.

It was short, but effective, not in terms of points scored but in team spirit stimulated. They lost the match but they felt that somehow the prayer at the beginning had a bonding effect on them. And Andrew had established himself as a credible Christian presence in the team.

This carried on into the Under-21 World Cup tournament a few months later. By the time the Irish team had travelled out to Argentina to play in the competition in June 2005 they all knew each other fairly well. Andrew had played with the Ulster guys like Stephen Ferris for most of the year and all the lads on the Irish team, whether from Ulster or not, knew what he stood for and respected his position.

They were scheduled to play four games in the group stages of the tournament, against Canada, France, Samoa and South Africa. When they were warming up for the first match Andrew made a very pleasing discovery. His teammates were actually expecting him to pray with them! What he had started in Wales after much prior personal prayer for strength and guidance was set to carry on as an anticipated item in the pre-match preparation before all Ireland's games in the World Cup.

As the players broke away from the cluster around Andrew to take up their positions for the kick-off just before their third game, one of the boys on the team remarked, "I like this praying before the match. It really gets me going for the game. Maybe we should start doing it at half-time as well!"

It was a good suggestion, but not one that was ever followed up, as the coach needed to make the most of his half-time team talk. It showed, though, what the guys thought of the pre-match prayer. They seemed to love it!

The Irish team won their matches against Canada and Samoa but were beaten by France and South Africa, which meant they were not set to progress any further than the group stages of the competition. Andrew had displayed his outstanding talents on the field, however, and this was soon to be rewarded by a call-up to the senior Ulster squad.

Andrew made his debut for the Ulster team on Friday, September 9, 2005, when still only twenty, against Cardiff at Cardiff Arms Park in the first Celtic league game of the new season. It was a thrill to have advanced to playing this level of rugby, and Andrew proved himself worthy of his place on the winning team.

It was just fifteen days later, on Saturday September 24 in the third match of the league that Andrew was to score his first Ulster try. The game was again away in Wales, this time against the Gwent Dragons at Rodney Parade, Newport.

The Dragons were leading by 16 points to nil well into the second half when Andrew crossed the line for the first time as a senior Ulster player. This try, when converted, marked the start of a remarkable comeback for Ulster and they finished up winning a very hard-fought game by a score of 19 –22. It was close, and Andrew had played a significant part in the victory.

An increasing awareness of this prodigious young talent on the rugby field was accompanied by a growing number of invitations to share his faith at youth events both in Ulster and beyond. One of the first of that season was when he appeared on a panel in a question and answer session at an evening with a sporting theme, in Coleraine Baptist Church. It was back to his home town, the town in which he had grown up and in which he had started to play his rugby.

Now, though, he was on a platform with Karen Humphreys, who had played hockey for Ulster, and was a sister of David, his boyhood hero whom he had joined on the Ulster team, and Nathan Mc Conville who played football with the Belfast club, Cliftonville.

The audience of young people were impressed to hear these sports stars talk about the practicalities of 'going for it all out,' not only as part of a team but also as people who were, as individuals, working towards a more noble, more rewarding and therefore more desirable goal. That was of being a shining example for Jesus Christ.

Andrew enjoyed that evening, as he did all the others where he was afforded the opportunity to talk about his Christian faith. He was never afraid to tell of the joy and peace it brought him in the duties and privileges of every day, whether that meant studying theology or training and playing with Ulster.

God loved him and Jesus had died for him and called him to be His child.

He had long since come to recognise, too, that it was God who had given him the physical gift he had as a sportsman. So was it not only natural that he should want to honour Him with his life, in everything he did, and everywhere he went?

# 5

# Savour The Moment!

WITH THE SUMMER over Andrew started back into training with the Ulster squad in preparation for the coming season. It was when arriving at the Newforge pitches in south Belfast for a session one afternoon in early autumn 2005 that he had an exciting, if somewhat unexpected, call on his mobile.

On answering it he found Gerard Carmody, manager of the Ireland rugby team, on the line. He had rung to invite the young Ulster player to 'come down to Dublin' the next week and train with the Irish squad in preparation for the three friendly matches coming up in November.

This was thrilling. He had gazed at the framed photo of David Humphreys in his Ireland shirt hundreds of times. Was he going to get his own shirt now? The manager hadn't been making any promises of a team place, but training with some of the internationals, who were up until then just names in a paper or pictures on a screen to him, would always be a start.

It was a start, too, but rather a daunting experience for the twenty-year old. He and Neil Best were the two 'new boys' from Ulster to join the squad and Andrew often felt like pinching himself to make sure he wasn't dreaming it all. When training alongside players who had represented their country dozens of times he thought more than once, 'what am I doing here? Do I really deserve to be among these guys?'

Andrew wasn't worried that he hadn't been selected to play in the first match of the three against New Zealand. He felt he was still 'finding his feet' in the squad and was happy to watch from the stand.

He was to receive a pleasant surprise, however, at the team talk on the Tuesday morning before next match against Australia on Saturday, November 19, 2005. Brian O'Driscoll was injured and Andrew had been picked to take his place in the centre. It was a great honour and as the week progressed Andrew trained with the thoroughness and enthusiasm for which he had become well known, and spent many quiet minutes, off the pitch and away from the others in silent prayer. This was what he had dreamt about as a boy, and now it was coming true.

On the afternoon of the match Andrew joined his new teammates for the pre-match warm-up and then when they returned to the dressing room for the final ten minutes before the match was due to start he sat down on one of the benches. Some of the other lads were chatting, some were having final strapping done, and some, were sitting leaning forward in silent contemplation. Reaching down Andrew slipped his Bible out of his bag, opened it at Psalm 84,and began to read. It had always been one of his favourite psalms and he found it encouraging that afternoon.

'Blessed is the man whose strength is in You...' he read.

'The Lord God is a sun and shield;
The Lord will give grace and glory...' it said farther down.

The last verse of the Psalm proclaimed with unmistakeable authority, 'O Lord of hosts, blessed is the man who trusts in You!'

That was exactly what Andrew was doing. Trusting in the Lord.

He replaced his Bible in his bag, bowed his head and asked God to help him on this big occasion. By this time the boys on the team were making for the door, It was almost time to go.

That was when Andrew had another unforgettable moment. David Humphreys, who had been his hero and role model from boyhood days, came over and said, "Enjoy the moment, Andrew. If you get a chance, take a good look around you before kick-off. There are well over 40,000 people out there!"

Those words of counsel and encouragement meant so much to the young player, about to run out on to the famous Lansdowne Road turf as an Irish player for the very first time. He wasn't long out either until he saw what David had meant. He did as he had been advised and took a moment to look up at the bank of people, stretching right up to the back of the towering stands. Many of these mad keen supporters had found innovative ways of bedecking themselves in the green of Ireland.

And the roar was deafening! 45,000 fired-up rugby fans can make a lot of noise!

It was a breathtaking experience. The support of the crowd for any positive Irish move was inspiring and Andrew felt he had made an acceptable if not spectacular impact on the game. The presence of David Humphreys in the team, and his timely advice had helped steady him before the match started and the interest of another world-class player allowed him to leave the pitch feeling very satisfied.

As the teams were making towards the dressing rooms after the final whistle Lote Tuqiri, a well-known figure in the Australian team, came across to the debutant.

"Well done Andrew. All the best," he said.

Andrew was pleased that he had even bothered to speak to him and was in the process of thanking him for the compliment when the Australian went on, "Here, would you like this to remind you of your international debut?" With that he pulled off his shirt and handed it to Andrew.

"I certainly would. Thank you," was the appreciative response.

It was another treasure to have framed and up on the wall among all the other bits and pieces in his growing collection of rugby 'stuff.'

That Australian match had been wonderful and Andrew was thankful to God for giving him the skill and the Irish selectors for giving him the chance to appear in such an important fixture. His performance must have pleased the team management too, for at the midweek team meeting he was told that he would be playing again the following Saturday, November 26, against Romania in another friendly at Lansdowne Road.

Thousands packed the stands once more and although the Romanians were not considered as rugby super-leaguers like the Wallabies, Andrew was delighted to be playing for his country once more. The sense of occasion wasn't quite so overwhelming for him second time around and he knew the routine.

He took time to read his Psalm between warm-up and kick-off and savoured the moment of taking the field in front of a huge and enthusiastic crowd yet again. It was hard to avoid thinking, 'are all these people here just to see us?'

When the game began, though, all sense of the unreal vanished. The crowd melted away into an encouraging background roar, and it was all to play for.

The atmosphere and his own gritty determination helped Andrew to show why the selectors had decided to give him a second game. He rewarded their confidence in him by contributing ten points with two tries in a winning score of 43 points to 12. It was an added thrill for him, too, when, in just his second match for Ireland, he was voted Man of the Match and presented with a trophy to mark this achievement. The young and rising star from Ulster had become a distant gleam on the international horizon.

When the Six Nations competition began in February 2006 Andrew sat out the first game against Italy but came off the bench to score a try in the second match against France in Paris. The atmosphere at end-to-end encounter was electric, with 80,000, mostly French, but all extremely passionate, fans packed into the Stade de France. The travelling Irish contingent were trying valiantly to make themselves heard in that cauldron of sound and Andrew's try gave them just cause for sustained vocal appreciation.

His notable performance in the French game resulted in him being rewarded with a starting place in the succeeding three matches in the Six Nations against Wales, Scotland and England. The final match of the tournament was at Twickenham in front of another huge and noisy crowd. This was Andrew's first appearance in an Ireland shirt at the English national stadium. Running out on to the pitch and lining up for the anthems was his sixth moment to savour.

Ireland won the match by 28 points to England's 24 that day, and the Triple Crown, as they had already defeated the other two 'home' nations in the earlier matches.

Andrew's talent in the team was becoming widely recognised and he signed a contract with Ireland in April 2006. The media coverage that had accompanied his having made six appearances for his country in five months led to the name of Andrew Trimble featuring regularly in the rugby press.

Further news reports were on the way too, for after a very successful season for Ulster in between international commitments, he was presented with the Ulster Senior Player of the Year Award for 2005–2006. This, coming as it did only three years after he had won the same title with Ulster Schools, was an indicator not only of the player's outstanding prowess on the pitch but also of his popularity with the fans and the press.

This growing public awareness led to Andrew, whose firm though never flamboyant Christian faith was an integral part of his lifestyle, becoming increasingly in demand as a speaker or panellist at events organised by schools or church youth groups.

When he began to hear of young people who had committed themselves to Christ as a result of these outings it gave him more, and different, moments to savour.

The treasures acquired on these occasions would never become discoloured or dusty. They were enduring and eternal and will ultimately go on display in his heavenly trophy cabinet.

# 6

# Introduce Yourself

HAVING BECOME ESTABLISHED in both the Ulster and Ireland team squads Andrew had one of his best games for his home province, in his home province, against the French side Toulouse, in the autumn of 2006.

Saturday, October 21 was a crisp sunny day and there was a feel-good factor abroad amongst the loyal crowd in Ravenhill. They were ready to roar on their team at every opportunity and they hadn't to wait long to be given one!

The fans were barely conscious that the game had even started when Andrew touched down in the third minute to score his first try of the afternoon. David Humphreys kicked the conversion and Ulster were 7 points ahead in just four minutes.

The home team played well right through the first half putting more points on the board before Andrew rounded it off by racing over the line with only a few minutes remaining to score his second try of the day. When this had been confirmed by the TV match official and the two points added for a successful conversion the Ravenhill faithful could barely believe what was happening!

Ulster went on to win the game by a score of 30 points to 3. The fans who had arrived hoping for, but possibly not really expecting, something special, left the ground with a lot to talk about. There could be no doubt either that the name of young Andrew Trimble, who had just celebrated his twenty-second birthday, would crop up in many of the lively discussions.

After playing regularly for Ulster through the season Andrew had an interesting meeting one evening after a match in the spring of 2007. Rico Tice, Associate Minister at All Souls, Langham Place, London, and co-author of the Christianity Explored series, came to the Ulster game at Ravenhill. He was visiting a friend in Northern Ireland and when he heard of Andrew and the Christian focus in his life, expressed an interest in spending some time with him.

As they chatted over a cup of coffee the renowned author and teacher told Andrew about the success, in terms of people contacted and lives committed to Christ, of the Christianity Explored series of Bible studies. It was, he said, an effective but non-threatening means of evangelism and a structure for explaining the Gospel.

The virtue of the studies lay in the fact that they allowed for personal interchange on what being a Christian really entails so that the person undertaking them could probe the subject as deeply as he or she wished. It was this importance of one-to-one sharing that Rico emphasised to Andrew. The young Ulster centre had, he said, created an excellent framework in which to share the message of Jesus with his teammates at all the levels in which he played rugby.

He suggested Andrew should build on that foundation not only by reading the Bible in the minutes before matches with other players around but also by taking every opportunity to share it with them. The Scriptures were the living Word of God he said, and if shared with the other guys, either in conversation or written form, God would use it, as and when He chose, to reveal Himself to them. All he expected of Andrew was to make sure he left it out there. It was like a seed that had to be sown to be of any use. It had to be in the soil, in a position where it could grow and bear fruit.

This was valuable counsel from an eminent Christian teacher and Andrew determined to act on it. He would continue to try to promote the Bible where possible and allow its message of truth and love to work on people's hearts and minds.

There were times when he would be presented, occasionally unexpectedly, with chances to talk about the Christian message. More than once he had players ask him, "Why do you read the Bible before matches Andrew? What good do you think that does you?"

This gave their teammate, whom they had all come to respect for his ability on the pitch, an opening to share his Christian faith. He explained that it helped him because he was in personal contact with an all-powerful God, to whom he could come as a son to his Heavenly Father, and was praying that his contribution to the game would be a credit to Him.

Andrew found himself in a strange situation when the Ireland rugby team were on a pre-World Cup tour of Argentina in May 2007. Many of the senior squad, the names that wrote themselves into the panel of thirty for France, were rested for the tour. This meant that younger players with some international experience like Andrew and Tommy Bowe were the 'old hands' and this left them feeling an added sense of responsibility.

Not only did Andrew have to wear Brian O Driscoll's number 13 shirt but he also felt that he ought to be a little more assertive on the pitch, and friendly to the new squad members off it. Eighteen months earlier he too had been new, and the already established players had been such an encouragement to him.

Now it was his turn to demonstrate an interest and concern, both as a player and a Christian, for the other lads on tour. This was a new role for Andrew and he discovered that it compelled him to think through, without becoming obsessed about, his tactics on the field and his attitude to those with whom he shared all the life situations they encountered, both as a group and individuals, on a daily basis.

The impact and influence of his prayer and Bible-reading interludes became obvious one day when the team was travelling between one match location and another in the South American country. Two of the men who were sitting together turned to Andrew and one of them enquired, "See when you are praying, Andrew. Do you ever pray for us?"

Gratified that they had identified him as someone who prayed, and assuming it to be a serious question, Andrew graced it with a sincere answer. "Occasionally," he replied in complete honesty, before going on to add, "But believe me I will from now on."

When he came to reflect on it after returning home Andrew looked back on his two weeks in Argentina as a character building exercise. He had learnt a few more things about himself, his game, and the effect simple Christian living could have on others when on tour.

During the summer of 2007 Andrew played in the World Cup warm-up game against Italy but wasn't selected for the match against Scotland on Saturday, August 11. That was all to change on the day though, for he was called on unexpectedly. The coach was anxious to see as many players as possible before the World Cup competition began in September and Andrew expected to be little more than a spectator at Murrayfield. He was helping out with some minor matters of administration and was just returning from a message to the ticket office when someone came looking for him. Shane Horgan had been injured and he was the only available replacement.

Although he hadn't thought he would be playing that day he had brought his boots with him to the ground 'just in case.' He was hastily kitted out in a team shirt and within minutes, on what was supposed to have been a 'rest' afternoon, he was running out on to the pitch. The sub who hadn't even been on the bench was soon into the flow of the game and had crossed the line for a try before the final whistle.

When it was suggested at the last training session that all the players travelling to the World Cup competition in France should bring something to give the other members of the squad as a keepsake, Andrew had one immediate thought. It was of Rico Tice and his advice.

Give them the Word of God.

How could he do anything better?

The team were due to assemble in Dublin on Monday September 3, and on the previous Friday Andrew asked a friend if he knew anyone in the Gideons, and told him why. He needed thirty Bibles, and he needed them soon.

Contact was made with one of the local branches of the organisation which distributes Bibles worldwide and they were thrilled to be able to help. Andrew had thirty beautifully bound presentation copies of the New Testament and Psalms delivered to him on Saturday morning!

On Tuesday evening the players exchanged what they had brought for one another in their Dublin hotel. Andrew handed out the copies of the New Testament and Psalms and these were gratefully accepted by all. In return Andrew was pleased to receive what the others gave him and the Irish team headed out to France the following day in good spirits.

Their confidence was to take a knock, however, when they were given a much tougher run than expected against what was perceived to be the weakest team in their group, Namibia. They won the game by 32 points to 17 but it hadn't been easy. Andrew scored a try during the game, his fourth in as many matches, having already gone over the line in the warm-ups against Italy, Scotland and Bayonne. The bad news was that he injured a finger during the game and this meant missing the following week's scrape-through win against Georgia.

The team were disappointed with these results for although they had won their first two matches narrowly they knew that tougher opposition lay ahead, in the form of France and Argentina. They had lost their confidence and when confidence is low teams don't as a rule play well, and when they don't play well confidence slumps even further.

In the middle of all the talks and training sessions aimed at somehow improving both the confidence and the performance of the team, Andrew noticed one encouraging sign. Some of the men were reading their New Testaments during the rest periods, and they weren't afraid to talk about it either!

Someone sitting in the corner of a lounge would call over to Andrew, "Hi Trimby, where would be the best place to start reading in this?"

There could be a number of different answers to this kind of query and Andrew usually directed the questioner, and there were a number who asked, to the 'help' section at the front. This listed the references for suggested verses to read when needing help in life situations. Andrew had a feeling that, given the mood in the camp, some of them would be likely to turn up the places recommended under the 'Depressed or Discouraged,' 'Failure Comes' or 'Feeling Inadequate,' headings. It was his prayer that with the interest some of the men were showing they would discover the 'Faith,' 'Forgiveness,' or Salvation,' sections.

His finger had healed sufficiently to allow him to play in the third group match, which was against the host nation, France, and on Thursday evening before the Friday game, Andrew was talking to Paul O' Connell, the much-capped Irish forward. In an attempt to encourage the younger player Paul remarked in the course of the conversation, "I believe you are going to introduce yourself to the world of rugby tomorrow, Trims."

Paul had obviously great confidence in the Ulster player's ability, and coming from someone of his standing in the game, Andrew took it as a sincere compliment, but the prophecy was not fulfilled. France dominated and won the match the next night to send Irish hearts even farther down towards their boots, and Andrew's personal performance was acceptable rather than notable.

An infection in his injured finger meant that Andrew had to be withdrawn from the team squad for the final match of the group stages against Argentina. Defeat in that game meant the Ireland team had failed to qualify for the knockout stages of the World Cup competition and were left with no other option but to return to Dublin.

When he arrived back home Andrew had time to recall and relive his experiences during a month in France. As he did this he thought often about Paul's prediction before the French game. 'You are going to introduce yourself to the world of rugby tomorrow.'

This gave him much food for thought. What Paul meant was that Andrew would make such an impact in his next game by Friday night every commentator and columnist in the rugby world would be singing his praises.

It hadn't happened.

Then he began to think of the story so far. He had represented Ulster more than 40 times, had 19 Irish caps and a cupboard full of Man of the Match and Player of the Year trophies. Had he not introduced himself to the world of rugby already?

In a sense he had, but there was another sense in which he hadn't.

He wasn't as well known as Jonah Lomu or Lote Tuqiri yet, nor would he ever aspire to be.

The lesson was that he still had a long way to go to be up there with the very best. He would have to keep 'going for it' and put in a lot of hard work before he could ever hope to introduce himself as a significant presence in the world of rugby.

Andrew is firmly convinced that God has led him into it, though, and he wants to do what's best for Him there, for as long as he is able to play.

Infinitely more important than introducing himself to the world of rugby is introducing as many people as he can to the love of Christ and the kingdom of God.

That's what he plans to be doing for many seasons to come.

# Going for it ...
## in a **wheelchair**

# Craig's
## Story

# 1

# Mum, Pray!

"MUM, pray!"

It was the urgent request of a son who knew his life was in danger.

The brief but urgent message came from Craig McMillan as he lay, totally unable to move, on the pitch at the end of a rugby match on Boxing Day 1999. He had been playing for Ballyclare High School 1 st XV and his team were winning. The final whistle couldn't have been more than five minutes away when he was spear-tackled into the ground.

Craig had grown up in a Christian home and trusted in Jesus as a young boy. Life for him until then had followed a pattern common to that of many Christian teenage boys. He went to church with his family, worked in school at the subjects he liked, and loved his sport. Up until that moment he appeared to have a bright future ahead of him as a rugby player, having already represented Ulster at schoolboy level.

The seventeen-year-old's parents and sister Emma had braved the cold of a midwinter day to come along to support him, but when Emma and mum Doreen began to feel the chill penetrate both clothes and skin they had returned to the car. That left dad, John, the sole family member on the touchline.

As the players started to leave the field in subdued and straggling groups to make towards the car park at what she had presumed was the end of the match, Doreen felt an inexplicable sense of foreboding. Craig didn't seem to be among them.

That was unusual, but perhaps he was coming with his dad, or perhaps they were both talking to somebody. They were bound to turn up soon.

Only one of them appeared, though. It was John.

The anxious father rushed across to the car and said, "Craig's on the ground!"

That had been enough to send mother Doreen and sister Emma hurrying back on to the pitch. When they reached the figure on the grass, a small group of people, including another parent who was also a nurse, had already gathered around him.

It was when Doreen knelt down beside her son that he had gasped his two-word prayer request. This had, in the fewest words possible, recognised the two most significant aspects of Craig's life, his family and his faith.

An ambulance had been called and the concerned bystanders covered Craig with coats to keep him warm while waiting for it to arrive. It was the reaction of the first paramedics to arrive on the scene that alerted the already distressed parents and sister to the real gravity of the situation. They wouldn't move Craig, opting rather to make him as comfortable as possible, and phone for assistance. A second ambulance was summoned and when the injured lad had been moved carefully into this vehicle it was given a police escort all the way to the Royal Victoria Hospital in Belfast.

The hospital staff had obviously been alerted by the incoming ambulance to the critical nature of the injuries sustained by the patient they were carrying, and reacted quickly. A consultant was called in and Craig was wheeled away to the theatre for assessment.

Meanwhile the news of Craig's accident had filtered out into the Christian community in the province, and stunned friends and relatives, wanting to do something, but unsure of what that should be, began to gather at the hospital. With Craig still in theatre and the extent of his injuries as yet unconfirmed, and everyone there numb with shock, they took what they considered to be the only appropriate course of action.

They convened an impromptu prayer meeting in a waiting area, which was otherwise unoccupied at that time of night. When lying critically injured Craig had begged his mum to pray, and she was doing that. Every breath and every sigh carried an earnest plea up to God that Craig, her lovely son, might live and not die.

Doreen couldn't bear all the burden of prayer alone, though. Nor would she be expected to. All those present in that waiting area prayed passionately for Craig, and for his mum, dad and sister who were totally traumatised by this turn of events in what had begun as a normal day in their family. They hardly knew what to say, or pray, but their Christian friends were able to feel their anguish and articulate their requests. Emergency prayer meetings had also been hastily arranged outside the hospital, in the Mountsandel Fellowship in Coleraine, and amongst other Christian groups. This was a time when everyone wanted to do what they could to help but all anyone could do was pray.

It was three o'clock in the morning before the hospital staff were in a position to give a detailed assessment of Craig's condition. The anxious parents, John and Doreen, asked their friend Dr. Wesley Magowan to accompany them to hear the news, and it was not good.

The consultant confirmed what must be any parent's worst nightmare. Craig's injuries were extremely severe. His neck was broken and his spinal cord had been completely severed. With these injuries he was likely to be paralysed for the remainder of his life.

Although they had suspected that Craig's injuries could be very serious from the moment they had seen the reaction of the paramedics on that field in Ballyclare, the word 'paralysed' hit John and Doreen McMillan like a hammer blow. Their big, strong, fit, handsome son who had appeared to have such a bright future both academically and as a sportsman, 'paralysed for the remainder of his life.'

It was a shocking, bewildering and totally devastating idea to have to try and accept. What were they going to do? And more importantly, what, if anything, was Craig ever going to be able to do again?

Having given the worried parents a complete and honest diagnosis of their son's current critical condition the consultant then went on to try and afford a crumb of comfort. He assured them that 'Craig was in the best possible place to receive the best possible treatment' and that he and his staff would do all they could for him.

The terribly-injured teenager lay in traction for the first three days, but when the medical team realised that this was not going to produce the expected result they decided to operate and insert rods to stabilise his neck. On the morning of the planned operation there was a problem, however. When Craig's mum and dad arrived into the hospital early to see him before he was due to go to theatre, the staff told them they couldn't operate because Craig's temperature had gone up. If it wasn't down by one o'clock in the afternoon, the vital operation couldn't be performed that day.

John and Doreen then resorted to what they had already discovered to be their most important resource, prayer. They phoned a number of their Christian friends, gave a brief outline of the situation, and asked them to pray. And it worked, too. God heard their petitions and intervened. Much instant and passionate prayer went up, Craig's temperature came down and the operation was carried out as scheduled.

After that essential surgery Craig was kept in intensive care for a number of days. His family spent long periods in hospital with him and as they saw their son and brother surrounded by all kinds of advanced medical gadgetry to keep him stable and monitor his condition they struggled to come to terms with it all mentally, emotionally and spiritually.

Sister Emma found it all very distressing and many nights cried herself to sleep. Craig was more than 'just a brother' to her. He was one of her best friends.

John struggled to keep himself from asking, Why? Craig had inherited his sporting ability, and they were united not only in their faith in Christ but also in their love of sport. They played golf together, skied together and trained together. Craig was more than just a son to John. He was his best mate.

What was going to happen now, though? Would Craig ever be able to sit up or stand up again? And that wasn't to mention catching a rugby ball or skiing down a mountain. What did the future hold?

His dad didn't even dare think about it. All he could do was pray.

A mother's dilemma was different again. She couldn't bear to see her son, who had once been so healthy and active, in such a state. It pained her unbearably. Although she couldn't ever imagine what life would be like without him there were times, in the darkest days of intensive care following the spinal operation that she found herself making a heartfelt plea to God. It was an earnest entreaty inspired by, but yet at the same time in constant conflict with, her strongest maternal instincts.

"Lord, " she prayed, "if Craig cannot be restored to some kind of a useful life, please just take him to be with Yourself now."

It was unbelievably difficult, and if his parents and sister found it traumatic how was Craig going to react if and when he recovered sufficiently to discover the full extent of his injuries?

The answer to that question came after he had been in hospital for ten days and was considered well enough to be moved out of intensive care and on to the fractures ward. That was when, after a long period of silent reflection he asked his mum who was beside his bed. "Tell me, what exactly is wrong with me?"

It was the moment and the question Doreen had been dreading, but knew that it had to come, and the issue had to be addressed and the truth told. Pausing for a few seconds to take a deep breath, and then trying to speak in a controlled voice despite a heart that was hurtling out of control, she replied, "Well, dear, you have broken your neck. And you will be paralysed to some degree for the rest of your life."

Craig, lying motionless in the bed, closed his eyes, bit his lip, and said nothing.

# 2

# Life For You Will Be What You Make It!

IT WAS COMING-to-terms time for Craig now too, but he didn't have time to worry about his condition or the future too long, before he was hit by a frightening setback.

One night in the fractures ward he experienced great difficulty in breathing and was rushed into intensive care once more. After a few hours on a ventilator he was able to breathe more easily and it seemed as if the difficulty had passed. It hadn't though.

There were occasions in those early days, after he had been told what the future would hold for him physically, and when he was having such problems with even getting a breath, that Craig began to feel insecure. Disturbing panic attacks left his mind in a whirl. Everything seemed so unpredictable. Once, when one of his lungs collapsed completely, he felt sure that he was about to die. What was this all about? Why was this happening? There were still the questions.

When Craig's parents came in each morning to begin another day's vigil in the hospital it was always with reports that people from all around the world were praying for him. Telephone calls that they had time to take, and voice-mail messages that had been left on their systems, from interested people, many of whom John and

Doreen had never met, told them that their family, or fellowship, or church, were 'all praying for Craig.'

Confirmation of this widespread concern amongst the Christian community afforded some measure of consolation to the perturbed mind in the paralysed body in the bed. It was reassuring. He had always been taught that we should bring 'everything to God in prayer.' His mind was so beset with anxiety that he was unable to articulate his requests to God, but others were doing it for him. That was great.

This mental insecurity, alleviated only by the realisation that thousands of people were talking to God about him, continued for a few restless days. He couldn't sleep, day or night. There was too much to worry about.

One afternoon, though, his mum was reading to him from the Bible. Craig was barely able to think straight never mind be in a position either mentally or physically to read anything and was missing out on his daily 'quiet times with God.' Recognising this, and also the importance of turning to the Word of God for comfort for both of them, Doreen had begun to read from the Scriptures every day at her son's bedside. There were particular passages that she turned to time and again, choosing them because she was sure that Craig would be familiar with the words and thus hopefully would derive some measure of encouragement from the sentiments they contained.

That particular day, as his mum's soft voice purred on from the chair beside the bed Craig felt an unusual sense of peace flood over him. The words seemed to have such a soothing effect... 'The Lord is my shepherd; I shall not want.

He maketh me to lie down in green pastures: he leadeth me beside the still waters.

He restoreth my soul: he leadeth me in the paths of righteousness for his name's sake.

Yea, though I walk through the valley of the shadow of death, I will fear no evil: for thou art with me; thy rod and thy staff they comfort me...'

What assurances! What consolation! He could rest in the Lord, whatever happened. The feeling of tranquillity that enfolded him saw all the tightness and tension evaporate from both mind and body and slowly he began to relax. He was soon in a deep sleep and slept soundly for hours for the first time in days.

The peace of God, which surpasses all understanding, had taken over, and Craig was enjoying the refreshing and restorative benefits of sleep.

Soon after that Craig's condition had improved sufficiently for him to be returned to the fractures ward yet again. He was told that he was to remain there until he was well enough to be transferred to Musgrave Park Hospital in south Belfast to commence rehabilitation. As part of the preparation for the move the medical staff were monitoring his breathing to make sure that he was physically ready for this next stage in his painfully slow progress towards what his mum had described in her earlier heartfelt plea to God as 'some kind of a useful life.' When they were satisfied that he was indeed fit enough for the transfer Craig's breathing tube was removed and he was medically ready to go.

He wasn't mentally ready to go, though. 'The Royal' had become his home, his safe haven, for the six weeks since his injury. He had begun to feel secure there. The staff all knew him and he felt comfortable with them around.

There could be no hanging back, though, and the day of the changeover was to prove a challenging experience for Craig and an emotional one for his mum.

Soon after he had been taken by ambulance on a spinal board the short distance between the two well-known Belfast hospitals and had been installed in a comfortable side ward in 'Musgrave Park' a consultant came to see him.

He was there to welcome Craig and to outline the programme of rehabilitation they were planning for him. His was no 'softly-softly, approach, however. It was a straightforward statement of fact and promise of help and support if Craig was willing to help himself.

"In case you didn't know it, Craig," he said, "You are never going to walk again. This isn't the end of everything,however. Life for you will be what you make it. We will teach you what you can do and support you in every way possible but it will be up to you to make the effort."

That was it in a nutshell. Rehabilitation would have to be a joint effort. After the consultant had gone Craig prayed that God would give him the determination to carry it through. If it could be done, he would certainly have a go at it.

When the other three members of the family arrived in at 'Musgrave' to see Craig established in his new surroundings, his mum broke down. It was the orderly line of wheelchairs waiting just inside the door of the ward that tugged at her heart. So this is what the future holds for all of us, she found it a struggle to admit.

Craig embarked on the prescribed programme of physiotherapy and occupational therapy with the words of the consultant ringing in his ears. 'Life for you will be what you make it.' It was hard at first but he persisted, backed up by expert and attentive medical and supportive care. Such were the extent of his injuries that rehabilitation meant the retraining of his entire body. When he found himself having to battle through the pain barrier time and again the staff informed him that the pain was coming from muscle loss but this would 'settle down if he kept at it.' Keeping at it was apparently all part of the 'it will be up to you to make the effort' package, and he would grit his teeth and get on with it.

His dogged desire to improve his quality of life to whatever it was that he was going 'to make it' was rewarded on his eighteenth birthday, March 1, 2000. That was the day when Craig made an almost superhuman effort of mind and body, and with the help of the staff in attendance sat up for the first time since the Boxing Day before. The exertion involved in performing what to a healthy body would be an intuitive action left him feeling weak and faint. It seemed as if all the blood had disappeared out of his head leaving it to spin sickeningly round and round.

The sense of satisfaction associated with this significant stepping-stone achievement more than compensated for the bout of dizziness, however. When he recovered after a short rest period he felt strangely excited to have started out on the road to wherever it was he was going.

Later that day Craig had yet another birthday treat. To mark his arrival in the world of the adult he had his first out-of-bed experience for more than two months.

During this time he made a trial run in an electric wheelchair.

# 3

# I Want To Push Myself!

IT WAS YET another milestone passed on the road to recovery, but what a momentous one!

Now Craig had managed to get out of bed and discovered that he was able to move about from one place to another. If he could operate an electric wheelchair using the hand and arm in which he had any power or feeling, his left, then perhaps he could do other things as well.

The mental fillip his first short trip in that electric wheelchair afforded him was exciting. The effort of making it, however, was physically exhausting. When he returned to his bed he was completely 'shattered.'

Next day it was out into the wheelchair again. Then he was into it the day after that and the day following that.

Craig had a target meeting each week with his consultant and a nurse. Their question always was, in the spirit of 'you will have to make the effort,' 'Where do you want to be in a week's time, Craig? How far do you think you can push yourself?'

The first target on which they all agreed was that Craig was to sit up in his wheelchair for two hours at a stretch, without fainting. This would sound simple to a healthy person, but it would definitely not be so easy for someone who had been lying flat for eight weeks. He had to learn to breathe again in an upright position, as his chest muscles had been paralysed, and his skin, which had become softer from more than two months in bed, had to become hardened to normal usage once more. The goals set by Craig's medical team represented only half of the targets he undertook to achieve, though. His mum and he would sit in the evenings discussing other less dramatic, but nonetheless extremely practical tasks to perform. The first of these was to learn to feed himself with his right hand.

Although he had less movement in his right hand, Craig wanted to bring it back into use again if possible. Instead, then of using his left hand, in which he would have more mobility, but which Craig considered unnatural, he persevered in trying to manipulate the cutlery with his right. Seeing he found it nearly impossible initially to hold anything in that hand, without even considering the control it would require to move something like a fork or a spoon with it, this was an uphill struggle.

His food became scattered around a bit during the first attempts but gradually more of it started to stay on the plate and then make it eventually to Craig's mouth. Dogged persistence was bringing a degree of dexterity to his right hand.

This was rewarding, if slow, progress.

As he continued to set himself new and often more taxing targets, Craig was encouraged by a constant quiet assurance that God was with him in his desire to push himself towards a meaningful lifestyle. During his parents' visits in the evening either mum or dad would read a passage from the Bible with him and Craig had a number of special verses, which he often requested. Two of these, from which he obtained great spiritual assurance and peace were, 'Be still and know that I am God,' Psalm 46; 10, and, 'Casting all your care upon Him, for he cares for you,' 1 Peter 5; 7.

Another factor which helped encourage Craig through his daily challenges was the constant stream of cards and letters that continued to pour in from all around the world. Many people, having heard of his accident, felt they ought to contact him, assuring him that he was in their thoughts and prayers.

The rugby fraternity, both in the province and beyond, were also very supportive. Craig had visits from David Humphreys, Gary Longwell, Trevor Ringland and Jonathan Bell, men who had once been his teenage heroes. These players, and others from the Ulster and Irish squads who made single visits, brought him in signed shirts to keep and also let him know what was happening on the rugby scene from week to week.

One particularly positive piece of news to reach him, as he was battling to return to what for him would be the optimum level of physical fitness, came from South Africa. Someone had been in touch to let him know that a Christian rugby team had heard of his accident through some friends in America. They were so affected by his story that they had begun to make Craig's rehabilitation a matter of prayer at all their training sessions.

Craig's next target was to be able to get down to the gym and start back on some kind of a training routine himself. He had been a very fit athlete when playing rugby and this was already proving beneficial in the rehab process. Before he could be admitted to the gym, though, he had to be able to sit up in his chair for at least four hours. This goal was reached about a week after he had achieved his two-hour target and so he was then ready for the gym.

On his first session in the gym he had an introductory consultation with the physiotherapists. They were able to tell Craig what he would be physically able to do. Some activities would be totally outside his scope, for example standing unaided or walking. There were many that he would be fit for and these were what Craig had to concentrate on. He wanted to push himself to the limit and so he set himself a couple of difficult and distant but eventually achievable targets.

The first of these was to lift his own body weight clear of an exercise plinth. He had been able to do this in rugby training six months before. Could he do it again? That was what he wanted to know. It would be worth giving it a try. This, if achieved, should equip him with the upper body strength to move himself sideways, using only his arms. When he had accomplished this he would be able to transfer from his wheelchair into bed or possibly even a car. It seemed a long way off, but it was something positive to work towards.

When the physios had discussed Craig's functional possibilities and limitations and agreed goals with him, then it was up to a team of occupational therapists to encourage him through the programme. Craig worked hard with them and his quiet, unquestioning determination to make the best of every gym period was inspirational. He was an example to others.

Every day saw him attempt to manage either heavier weights or more repetitions. Each new challenge was met with renewed enthusiasm. If life for him was going to be what he made it, he was determined, with the help of God and the support of a caring family and attentive professionals, to make it good.

A further incentive to make the best of his situation came in almost daily reports from 'outside' on the progress of The Craig McMillan Fund. Shortly after his accident on the school rugby field and the serious nature of his injuries became known, the staff and pupils of Ballyclare High School established this Fund to raise finances to help with Craig's rehabilitation. He was constantly amazed when his mum, who taught in the school, told him about generous donations to, and willing collections by all kinds of groups and individuals for, the Fund. Craig felt grateful to those who had the vision of care to initiate the Fund, those who had the commitment to carry it on, and most of all to God for this provision, through the enterprise of ultra-caring people, for his welfare.

One of the first items which could be procured through the Craig McMillan Fund was a new personal wheelchair. With Craig making steady progress in rehab the time was fast approaching when he would be discharged from hospital. He would have access to a hospital chair but preferred instead to have a lightweight model manufactured to meet his specific needs.

This led to Craig having to make a decision at the beginning of May as to what kind of wheelchair he would like to use. Having tried both an electric wheelchair, and when his arms became strong enough to use it, a manual one, Craig opted to gear himself towards using a manual chair.

His decision gave the concept of pushing himself a totally new meaning. Not only was he pushing himself to attain the highest fitness level possible but moving from one spot to another was also going to entail pushing himself in another sense, physically with his own two hands!

When asked why he thought it better to use a manual chair Craig explained to those who were a little surprised at his choice that there were two reasons for it. The first was that it was probably a question of self-esteem. Attaining and maintaining peak physical fitness had been a hobby, almost a fixation with him, throughout his teenage years. A manual chair was the more 'active' option, as it actually allowed 'mobility' to become part of Craig's daily training schedule.

There was a second very practical reason why Craig chose to use a manual wheelchair. It would be more transportable. A manual chair could be folded down and stored in a car boot making travel with the family and friends much easier. An electric chair could only be carried in a specially adapted vehicle with ramps or hoists.

As soon as he had stated his preference for a manual wheelchair Craig began using one of the chairs in the hospital. This proved to be quite a challenge for not only was it an acquired skill that had to be perfected but he also found the chair to be heavy and much harder to push than he had expected. He accepted this as being all part of the learning process and hoped the chair he had been measured for and which would be ready before he was well enough to leave hospital would prove lighter and more manageable.

By mid-June Craig was pushing himself around with comparative ease but he had modified the chair to help make this possible. Having asked his dad to bring him in a couple of old tubes out of bicycle tyres, father and son then cut them and attached them to the push-rim of the chair to allow him to grip it more easily.

This wasn't Craig's only 'invention' either. He had become fed up with picking up little wooden cubes and trying to set them one on top of the other after four or five weeks of it, and struggling to write the alphabet endlessly. There must be other things he could do.

He and his mum discussed his inability to write because he couldn't hold a pen properly and Craig suggested that he could modify some devices that had already been designed and approved, gearing them towards his own specific needs. He was thinking of something that would clip onto the side of his hand. This gadget would have a hole in the portion that rested in the palm of his hand. When a pen was slipped into this hole he could close his fingers on it to a certain extent and thus he should be able to write.

The idea was good, and after they had discussed it at length and a few prototypes were made, Craig came up with what for him was the perfect design. It worked! He could write with it, as he remarked to someone with a laugh, 'as well as I was ever able to write.'

This success inspired him towards considering developing the concept. What if he were to design one for the other hand as well? Could he hold a set of pens or 'sticks' made of some other rigid material and use them to press down the keys on a computer keyboard? If that could be done then he would be able to use his computer again!

One evening as they sat chatting about the clip device Craig was using to hold the pen, and with which he was becoming slowly more proficient at writing, his mum enquired, "What about working on your teeth now, Craig? Could you manage a toothbrush, do you think? Away in there to the bathroom and try and brush your teeth."

Another question had raised a further possibility and as far as Craig was concerned it merited an attempt. This time it wasn't food all over the floor that was the problem as it had been with the initial 'feed yourself with your right hand' instruction. It was more toothpaste all over his face! Craig persisted, however, and with his toothbrush slipped into a holding strap he had, within days, fine-tuned the art of brushing his teeth.

In early July a couple of nurses from the Musgrave who had been on courses with Back-up, a sports charity for people with spinal injuries, suggested to Craig that he might enjoy going to a Back-up Outdoor Camp. They had been impressed by his determination to push himself to the limit in every aspect of life and reckoned that he was the kind of person who would benefit from such a course.

It gave Craig a boost to realise that he wouldn't be leaving hospital just to sit around in a corner in a wheelchair. If the nurses were to be believed there were lots of activities in which, with his will and sense of purpose, he could become most enjoyably and profitably engaged. With this thought in mind he applied to attend the course.

His discharge from hospital at the end of July was yet another landmark on the torturous journey back towards 'some kind of useful life.' It was great to be back in the family home again outside Ballyclare and to see the building work that was already well advanced towards providing him with specially designed living accommodation 'out the back.'

The Back-up course, which was held in the English Lake District in mid-August turned out to be a real confidence boost for Craig. When there he participated in a wide range of activities. These included mountain climbing, sailing in a mini-catamaran and abseiling over a cliff. If anyone had told Craig six months before that he would be attempting such things he would have said they were crazy.

Although he couldn't walk up the mountain he was pushed up it. He was pulled up it. He sat in a special chair and was manhandled up it. It was tough going at times. The point of it all was that he reached the top!

Before the end of the week Craig had learnt the lesson that the course had been created to teach. It was that he wasn't made of glass. He wasn't going to break. His body was still tough. He could still push himself to the limit, fall, and survive.

Every morning, before embarking on the strenuous programme mapped out for that day, he would pray to God for guidance and protection, and then trust himself to his tutors. As he was preparing to abseil over the cliff he was gripped by a moment's trepidation.

What happens if I fall here? he wondered.

This thought was soon replaced by another. It was simply, 'What's the worst thing that can happen here? I have already broken my neck. What, other than death itself, could be worse than that? Hurry up. Get on with it!'

In the middle of that week, which was to prove such a physical challenge and moral encouragement to Craig he found himself having to ponder another question. It was, what happens next?

Where do we go from here?

What happens when I get back home?

This issue had been raised by the fact that the coursework results for his A-level subjects, as much of it as he had been able to complete before Christmas had come in. He had done well in it. His mum was keen that he return to school in September and repeat his A-level year.

How could he, though, go back to school in a wheelchair? A school where half the classrooms were upstairs?

There was another thing Craig thought about too. All the mates with whom he had come up through school had left in June. He would have to make new friends.

Should he go back to Ballyclare High School?

And if he didn't, what should he do?

What could he do?

# 4

# We Will Be Very Pleased To Have You!

THE ANSWER WAS that he could continue to live an active life. This meant simply carrying on from where he had been forced to leave off eight months earlier.

Having spoken to the Headmaster of Ballyclare High School, who promised to do whatever he possibly could to facilitate him, Craig decided to follow his mum's counsel and return to repeat his A – level year. It was a new experience to be driven to school every day, and then wheeled to classes, but Craig soon adjusted. He approached the prospect of another year back in class with a positive attitude. There was no escaping the reality that life was still only going to be what he made it, and he was totally determined to make the most of it.

The school management made, as they had promised, whatever changes were necessary to help him settle into the learning environment once more. All his classes were timetabled to downstairs classrooms, and as he was unable to make it to the Upper Sixth common room upstairs he was provided with his own personal study room on the ground floor. Although Craig was becoming increasingly proficient with the pen-in-the-clip he was still unable to write quickly enough to take notes in class so he was assigned a 'scribe' who took notes for him.

He needn't have worried either about his old mates having left school to progress into employment or tertiary education. Within weeks of returning to school he had acquired many new friends, some of whom although younger, had been on the same teams as himself and so they already knew one another. Also the unique nature of his situation and his cheerful acceptance of it attracted many to his side

When he was well settled into the school routine Craig felt that it was time to return to his spiritual home. By mid-September he was ready to go back to Mountsandel Christian Fellowship.

There were tears in many eyes that Sunday morning as he wheeled himself in. His church family were overjoyed to see him again. They there had been praying for him right from the night of his accident, and following the various stages of his treatment and improvement with great interest.

Now here he was. His life had been spared, in answer to the passionate prayers of that first night, and he had come back, in person, to see them.

When the pastor had welcomed him on behalf of the church fellowship, Craig was asked if he would like to 'say a few words.' He would, but it was only 'a few words.' He said how much it meant to him to be back with them and thanked them for their prayers and all their other expressions of concern. Craig also praised the skill of the medical teams both in the Royal and Musgrave Park but he gave the overall credit for his recovery so far to God. It was He who had heard the thousands of prayers on his behalf and answered them in a way that on occasions transcended medical expectations.

Having Craig back amongst them also proved a great encouragement to the staff and pupils of Ballyclare High School and provided them with a practical example of how the money they had collected through the Craig McMillan Fund had been put to good use. This spurred the organisers on to greater things. It was obvious that as Craig moved out to take his place in the community once more he would discover that there were other needs to be met. They resolved to make another big fundraising effort to help provide these necessities.

Those of the staff and pupils who followed the fortunes of the Irish Rugby team had learnt from their autumn fixtures list that the national side were due to host South Africa in November. Recognising that this could represent an ideal opportunity to make a significant one-off collection they approached the Irish Rugby Football Union with a specific request. Although they knew that many IRFU members were already aware of Craig's injury they stated his position yet again in writing and asked for special permission to make a collection at the game.

This was granted without hesitation and the IRFU volunteered to take the matter a step further by offering to mention the collection for the Craig McMillan Fund in the match programme and announce it over the PA system on the afternoon of the game.

Craig and his dad had been ardent supporters of the Irish rugby team for years, travelling together to all their home matches in Dublin. It was strange to be back there again, about a year since they had last watched an international together, with Craig being given special treatment, having been accorded the unwished-for status of 'injured player.'

It was also a little unnerving and very humbling to notice, as he was driven up to the famous Lansdowne Road ground, a team of collectors with buckets outside the gates. They had the words Craig McMillan Fund emblazoned across bright yellow T-shirts and seemed to be very busy. They were all around the ground, too, Craig was soon to discover, stationed at strategic points of entry. Grateful to be allowed to make a collection at such a high-profile match the organisers made the most of the opportunity. They had brought a busload of volunteer collectors, both staff and senior pupils, down from Ballyclare for the occasion!

As he sat in his wheelchair beside a number of other 'injured players' before kick-off Craig felt a sense of satisfaction and gratitude to God, and all those who had been willing to make a collection on his behalf, sweep over him. It was great just to be able to be near the touchline of an international rugby match again. The fact that Ireland lost the match in the end by a score of 18 points to South Africa's 28 detracted only slightly from the thrill of being 'at Lansdowne' once more.

If his eighteenth birthday treat had been his first ride in an electric wheelchair Craig's Christmas present for the year 2000 was to take possession of the new, specially fitted-out apartment at the rear of his parents' home. His dad, who was in the construction industry, had seen to it that the building work progressed with all due haste and Craig was given the keys and moved into it on Christmas Day.

With no rugby matches to play or training sessions to attend Craig spent the winter months doing what he hadn't done specifically during the start of his previous A-level year. That was concentrating on his studies. He was determined to make something worthwhile of his life despite the physical restrictions imposed by his disability.

In early March 2001 he was invited to be the guest speaker at a meal as part of a week of Gospel outreach at the GLO Centre in Motherwell, Scotland. This was to be the first time Craig had been put in a position where he would be expected to express how he felt about his physical condition and life situation since Boxing Day 1999, and he accepted the invitation with slight trepidation.

It worked out to be much less of an ordeal than he had anticipated, however, for the questions were being posed by John Speirs, director of Gospel Literature Outreach and a close family friend who had been following Craig's progress for the previous fifteen months with constant prayerful concern. An attentive audience listened, intrigued, as Craig recounted, in response to John's probing, how he had felt during those first dark days in hospital. He went on to tell how he had become so conscious of the peace and presence of God with him, initially in his fight for life and subsequently in his struggle to come to terms with his new style of life. The answer to his final question gave praise to God for preserving his life and providing him with a caring family and kind friends all of whom had 'gone the second mile, in doing what they could to make sure he had everything he needed.

That meeting was to prove a blessing both to those who had come to hear what Craig had to say, and to the speaker himself. The listeners couldn't help but be impressed by the quiet godliness and unaffected graciousness of this young man. He appeared to be accepting what they would have considered 'a tragedy' as an intervention of God in his life.

They had got it right. He was, too. That's how Craig was coming to regard his position. When he began to reflect on the meeting and the appreciative reaction of those who spoke to him after it he was able to come up with an answer to the question of 'why has this happened to me?' The teenage, training, sporting Craig would never have considered himself a public speaker and yet that evening he had been sitting in his wheelchair talking openly and confidently about his implicit faith in God.

During the spring and summer of 2001 Craig found a series of Bible studies arranged by Brian Haugh from Carrickfergus, a friend from Glenabbey Christian Fellowship, a helpful spiritual focus. Craig knew Brian's son and daughter well and this man had a genuine interest in teaching a group of young people the basic principles of Christian living, from the scriptures.

The programme was structured so that all those participating had material to read and subjects to think about in preparation for the next meeting. This preliminary reading and reflection pressed Craig into studying in depth what the Bible taught on a number of topical issues relating to living as an effective Christian in an unsympathetic society. The opportunity to discuss these matters with up to ten others of his own age in the informal setting of the Haugh home then afforded him the opportunity to voice his opinions in a congenial atmosphere.

It wasn't until later that Craig realised the benefits of this experience. These were that it had allowed him to identify, and then express what it was that he actually believed about, a range of spiritual topics he had never studied in depth before. This was to serve as a stabilising and maturing influence on his Christian faith.

When faced with completing a University application form during his A-level year Craig considered a number of options and decided to apply for a course in Construction Engineering and Management at the University of Ulster, Jordanstown. He was anxious to carry on a family tradition in construction, but some people considered it a peculiar choice. They fully understood why Craig should want to enrol on this course but wondered how a guy in a wheelchair would cope in what they had assumed to be an essentially practical subject. And when he graduated how could he possibly pursue a career in it?

Acceptance to his chosen course was dependent on attaining certain grades in his A-level examinations and when the results came out in August Craig's three 'B's' exceeded the stated entry requirements. When he was invited to attend the University for an interview Craig was concerned in case he would be refused admission to the Construction Engineering and Management Course because of his disability.

He hadn't been in with Sam McCaughey, the course director, long, however, until he discovered that any misgivings he had were totally ill-founded. His attitude was not one of 'do you think you can cope with all the demands of the various aspects of this course?' but rather, 'are there any changes we need to make? What can we do to make things easier for you?'

At one point Craig began to attempt to express his initial reservations by saying, "I had thought that seeing I am in a wheelchair it would be difficult for…"

The course director refused to allow him to even finish the sentence. His immediate reaction in response to that idea was most reassuring.

"Don't even consider anything like that, Craig," he interrupted. "We will be very pleased to have you!"

# 5

# First Class

HOW AM I going to get there?

And, how am I going to fit in and make my way around the place when I do?

These are the two questions often uppermost in the mind of someone with a disability when starting a new school or other institute of learning or commencing work in a new environment.

During Craig's A-level year these issues had been adequately addressed not only by him but also by his family and the headmaster and staff of Ballyclare High School. The school had made every provision they possibly could for him and by Easter he was driving himself to his studies.

This was only possible because in March 2001, shortly after his nineteenth birthday, he took possession of another 'set of wheels.' Having had his first ride in an electric wheelchair for his eighteenth, a year's determined progress saw him behind the wheel of a specially adapted Ford Focus.

Craig had been driving a normal manual car before his accident, but now he was able to drive this automatic model that had been fitted out taking into account the nature of his injuries and his limited physical capabilities. Since he had no power at all in his legs or feet Craig's new motor had a pin on the steering wheel to help him grip it and both accelerator and brake on the same lever attached to the steering column. He needed assistance in transferring from his chair to the car at first, but that is what he had been training towards in developing his upper body strength and the prospect of being able to travel independently again spurred him on to overcoming all, what were to him minor, obstacles.

Just before commencing his degree course Craig was invited to meet the Disability Officer and Course Director from the University of Ulster. They had catered for students with varying levels of disability before but none of them had been studying engineering. Their prime concern therefore was to ensure that Craig would find all parts of the campus where he would be expected to attend lectures or tutorials, accessible.

Aware that this incoming first year student would be needing help both in making his way around the university campus and making notes in lectures the Disability Officer arranged for him to have a helper to accompany him throughout the day. This person met Craig when he arrived in the morning and went with him to take notes at his direction. As he became used to the system and as he continued to perfect his proficiency with the pen, Craig learnt how to back up his 'scribe's' notes by making a few meaningful headline jottings of his own. This helped him recollect the significance of the material when he came to review it at a later date.

In early January 2002, during the Christmas vacation, Craig set off on what was to be one of the most exhilarating adventures he had experienced since his accident. When in the Lake District on the activity holiday with Back-Up some eighteen months earlier he had applied to go skiing with a small group of people in wheelchairs. He had always enjoyed skiing holidays with the family during his teenage years and fancied returning to the slopes to have a go in a 'ski cart.'

Craig had been pleased to be granted a place on the 2002 trip and then to meet up with the other seven prospective sit-skiers and eight attendants at London's Heathrow airport en route to Sweden. Each of the wheelchair-bound guys was assigned his own personal assistant, for although they were all experts in pushing their own chairs on dry ground pushing them in snow was a different matter entirely! That was just one of the occasions when the assistants proved their indispensable status by tipping the chairs onto their back wheels.

Preparing to go out for their first morning's skiing turned out to be quite a struggle, but also a genuine source of amusement, for all the would be skiers anxious to be whizzing down a mountain. As most of them had no movement in their lower limbs they had to wear layer upon layer of protective clothing and watching eight disabled men wrestling to get this on was quite a spectacle. Some of them ended up begging for a rest before going out and on to the next stage of the morning. They declared themselves 'knackered' before they even started!

Before going up in the ski lift each man had to be transferred out of his chair into a ski-cart and strapped in. They were replacing day mobility with snow mobility. Having been taken up in the lift they were given some basic instruction on the operation of the ski-cart and then they were off, one by one, down the piste.

Craig found this a fantastic experience. Zipping through freezing air with powdered snow stinging his cheeks and spattering his goggles he felt as he had never done before on a ski-slope. He was close to the ground, travelling faster that he had ever done independently and out of his car for two years. The sky was blue, the snow was white, the air was clear, the mountain scenery was stunning and he was at one with it all.

His excitement was verging on euphoria. He was overwhelmed by a tremendous sense of freedom. It was like leaving the world behind and entering a realm where nothing existed but a sensation of speed, the glint of sun on snow and a phenomenal affinity between himself and his Heavenly Father, the God of creation.

As with the Back-up activity week in the Lake district so with the sit-skiing holiday in Sweden. There were lessons to be learnt and Craig was an eager student. Most of these were to do mainly with his reactions and capabilities. The initial revelation came early in the week when a subconscious awareness began to alert him to the fact that he had actually begun to enjoy himself again. I am engaged in sport and actually loving it, he thought. This is what I did for most of the early part of my life and now I am back at it again! With that delight in recreation came an urge to push his body and mind to the limits once more. Craig was never content just to cruise down the mountain and then make it back up to the top and do the same again. It was always how much faster can I go? Or how much farther?

Spending the week with seven other blokes in wheelchairs had wonderful, while often subliminal, benefits too. The eight of them, all together because they were all disabled, but yet all wanted to be out there engaging in challenging physical activity, learnt so much from each other. It was amazing how many tips on technique were shared among the group either vocally through conversation or more often than not simply silently through observation. These could range from anything to negotiating obstacles in wheelchairs or the most hassle-free method of getting into, and then out of when they were wet, those layers of leggings!

That week in Sweden had been such a rewarding experience that Craig was only home a few days until he had his application sent off to go again the following year. Places on the course were very limited and demand far exceeded possible provision so Craig was pleased when he was awarded a place for the second year running. This was unusual but there were two factors in his favour. The first of these was that he was an experienced skier having been proficient at the sport before December 1999 and then he had been impressive on the ski-cart at his first attempt. With this background he could be depended upon to help encourage and coach the newcomers.

The other reason he was allowed to go a second year was that he was hoping to gain a higher-grade licence, which would be recognition of further achievement. He was successful in this quest on his second year out and was awarded the licence, but then he had to retire to free up places for others!

As news of Craig's positive attitude and unswerving faith was reported in occasional newspaper features, and spread by word of mouth amongst the Christian community in Northern Ireland, he continued to be invited to speak at various church and youth events from time to time.

On one of these occasions he was asked to share his experiences with the Women's Group in his home church, Mountsandel Christian Fellowship. This was different from most of all his other engagements, however, in that his mum, Doreen, had also been invited to take part. After Craig had been interviewed, many of those who were present, and who had been very close to the situation as it had unfolded, were touched as she told what it was like to have gone through the trauma of the previous couple of years as a Christian mother.

Scripture Union and Crown Jesus Ministries recorded his testimony on video as part of a visual presentation in their Power to Change outreach programme and this was widely distributed. Then on April 19, 2003, Easter Saturday, he was interviewed live for a radio programme being produced and broadcast by Emmanuel Baptist Church, Lisburn.

Craig approached this broadcast opportunity with a sense of responsibility and prayed that God would lead him as to what he should say in response to the questions he would be asked. His concern for the radio interview was the same as it had been for the video recording. He didn't want it to be focusing undue attention on him but rather what God had done for, and hopefully would see done through, him.

His prayers were answered for when he was in front of the camera or the mike he was enabled to relate not only what had happened but also how his faith in God had helped him cope during his stay in hospital and subsequent rehab. He was also able to bring the situation right up to date by telling how he felt that God was guiding him in his present position as a university undergraduate.

It was during his second year at university also Craig discovered another sport which he would gradually come to love. That was wheelchair rugby. In the autumn term he had travelled south to Dublin to watch Ireland's main team in the sport, the Gaelic Warriors, play and he liked it.

The physical element of it, all the bashing and bumping to try and gain possession of the ball by robbing one's opponent of it, appealed to him. As far as he could see, although played in a sports hall rather than on a field, and in specially designed and protected wheelchairs rather than by running and rucking, it was as near as it was possible to get to 'the real thing.' That was the game in which he had already represented his province and in which he had once begun to dream of representing his country.

He started attending the training sessions in Dublin with the Warriors and was then selected to play on the team of eight in the National Championships in London. This was another new and completely revitalising experience. Sit skiing had allowed him to feel the buzz of participating in a sporting activity but it was an individual non-contact, apart from the occasional tree, sport. Here he was now playing an actual team game in which one had to score points to win matches!

Although using a borrowed chair in which he, as 'the new boy on the block,' seemed to be singled out for a merciless hammering, Craig loved it. The sheer aggression of it, with the mounting urge to 'give as good as he got' had him wanting to play in every match possible. He almost managed that too, for the rules stated that the team of four players on the court at any one time could not exceed an 'eight-point rating.' Since Craig had been classified with a low-point rating it meant that he could play a specific role on the court. He was also rapidly developing his understanding of the game, and was playing, and pounded, for most of the tournament.

Having established himself in the Gaelic Warriors team, and possessed of an ardent desire to continue his involvement with wheelchair rugby, Craig had a sports chair made to measure. When this arrived in the late spring of 2003, having been manufactured by a firm of specialists in New Zealand, he became even more enthusiastic about the sport. Although all of his training sessions were in Dublin, and some of them took place during university term time, Craig made it to most of them. His course director, on learning of his ability at, and wishing to endorse his passion for, the game, granted him leave of absence to attend.

With the third year of his university course due to be spent out on placement with an employer Craig was faced with another first. He had applied to a number of companies from a list supplied by his tutors in the engineering faculty at the University of Ulster and was invited to attend for his first job interview.

Preparing for this placed him in a position where he was compelled to reflect on his capabilities and how he could promote them. It also, however, had him reflecting on his limitations and what would happen about them.

How, for example, would the board of directors of an engineering company react to a prospective employee turning up for interview in a wheelchair? Was his disability going to prove a disadvantage?

He attended the interview with the planning division of the Eastern Health and Social Services Board in Belfast on the appointed date and was pleasantly surprised that the fact that he was in a wheelchair didn't appear to have been an issue. About a week later Craig was notified that his application for the position had been successful and the letter included a starting date.

It would have been difficult to dream up a job more suited to an engineer in a wheelchair than that one. Craig's brief was to work with the Board on the design and layout of its health care buildings and there was surely no one better equipped to evaluate them for disability access than him. He was able to visualise moving through hospitals or health care buildings in his wheelchair, or indeed on a bed, and it would soon become clear what changes needed to be made to the design.

Craig was only a few months into his 'year out' when he began to appreciate that this was a most acceptable way to 'study.' There were no long evenings of bookwork, no lectures to be attended and no notes to be taken. He worked from nine to five at something where he felt uniquely qualified to make a significant contribution, then went home in the evenings to relax at whatever took his fancy and to crown it all he was being paid for the whole experience!

At the end of the academic year he compiled a report on the value of his placement for his university tutors and his employers were also asked to submit an assessment of his performance in the workplace.

During the opening weeks of his fourth year Craig gave a presentation on his year spent in the world of work. The other students then questioned him on it, as he was also allowed to grill them when their day for presentation came around.

Craig worked very hard at his studies during the final year. He enjoyed the subject and the evenings that were not taken up with trips out to occasional speaking engagements with a church or youth group somewhere or training sessions in Dublin with the Gaelic Warriors were spent in concentrated study.

It paid off too, for when results of the final examinations were posted in June 2005 Craig was one of only three from his course to be awarded First Class honours in his degree.

Graduation Day was a proud occasion for the family. Dad John, mum Doreen and sister Emma all found it hard to hold back the tears as Craig wheeled himself forward to have his degree conferred. They could never have imagined, that cold raw Boxing Day four and a half years earlier, when they had seen him lying, fighting for life on a field in Ballyclare, that this moment of glory lay ahead.

Nor could the consultant, who predicted that life for him would be what he made it, ever have visualised what he would 'make of it.'

He had, through sheer determination and with the help of God, the support of his adoring family, the prayers of hundreds of friends and the attentive tuition of the teaching staff at Ballyclare High School and the lecturers and tutors from the University of Ulster, made it big.

He had made it all the way up into First Class.

# 6

# Just Like It Used To Be!

AFTER ALL THE excitement and well-deserved congratulations of the graduation Craig began to consider finding employment. Being in a wheelchair hadn't stopped him from going to university and completing his degree.

Would it hinder him getting a job though?

During the summer after he graduated he sent off a few application forms and if he heard anything at all in response it was the thanks-but-no-thanks letter that thanked him that for his application and informed him in virtually the same sentence that 'the position had now been filled.'

This didn't worry him particularly at first. He hadn't been all that keen to go straight into full-time work after graduating but filling in application forms seemed like the accepted thing to do. If he had been appointed somewhere in the summer it could have turned out to be a drawback to him as he had something else on his mind.

Wheelchair rugby.

The European Wheelchair Rugby Championships were due to be held in Denmark in mid-October 2005 and Craig, who had become an established player with the Gaelic Warriors, seemed set to be selected for the Irish team. He trained hard over the summer, both in a mini-gym at home and in training sessions in Dublin, and was delighted to earn his place on the team representing Ireland.

Pulling on an Ireland shirt for the first time was a particular thrill for Craig. From representing Ulster in the field game he had always dreamt of playing for his country. That hadn't been possible, but now he was fulfilling his ambition in the wheelchair version and it was very special.

When he went out to play his first match of the tournament against the defending champions, Great Britain, he realised that this was wheelchair rugby up a few levels from anything he had ever played before. The opposing team had picked out this new player for Ireland as a potential weak spot and they gave Craig a ruthless battering. He didn't mind that. He was playing for his country and he was going to give it his best shot. Great Britain, who were favourites for, and eventually went on to win, the championships ran out winners of that opening match, but again Craig didn't mind. That was to be expected.

There were twelve teams competing in the tournament and with five matches in the initial pool games and then two 'crossovers' Craig played seven matches all in the space of an action-packed four days. When all the matches were played Ireland ended up in the bottom half of the league but for Craig it had been a memorable experience and one he would look forward to repeating two years down the line, if he could keep fit, and be selected.

Arriving back in Northern Ireland after the championships brought with it a sense of anticlimax. Suddenly, after all the heights and peaks of excitement in the competition period everything had gone horribly flat.

The games had been great. The camaraderie in the team and the rivalry with the other competitors had been inspirational. There were even times when Craig was able to share his faith with those he had come to know best.

Now all that was gone. The buzz had died.

It was November. The days were becoming shorter and seemingly endlessly wet.

Craig was alone in his apartment for the greater part of the day with the rest of the family out at work. There were a few training sessions to attend with the Gaelic Warriors but these were few and far between. Everybody seemed to be taking a break from wheelchair rugby except the professionals, and he wasn't a professional.

There were occasional bright spots amongst dark days and these came with the visits of his grandfather, whose surname, Craig, had become his Christian name. 'Papa' would appear just before lunchtime, prepare something to eat for both of them and then they would chat over the meal and on into the afternoon. The young man enjoyed listening to his grandfather recount some of his experiences in the family business or when out taking part in Gospel missions. They discussed a wide range of topics together, ranging from Craig's current sporting activities to politics, and from holidays they had enjoyed abroad to thoughts from the Bible they had enjoyed in their 'quiet times' at home.

One of these 'gems from Papa Jim' helped Craig immensely, allowing him to put things into some kind of perspective. Granda had been talking about a message he had given during one of his many preaching engagements on the theme of 'joy' in the book of Philippians in the Bible.

In the course of his remarks he asked, "Do you know the difference between joy and happiness?"

When Craig confessed that he had never really thought about it Papa went on to explain that, "Happiness is something that everybody craves but few achieve and even when they have it they can't keep it. Joy, on the other hand, is something that the Christian has, deep in his heart, and he never loses. Happiness, you see, depends on happenings but joy depends on Christ."

That was it. Craig often drew strength to keep going when he recalled these words. He still had Christ to guide him, and that would make all the difference.

Through all these days one thought was always uppermost in his mind. It was, when am I ever going to get a job? He had sent away more application forms and had been called for interview on a couple of occasions, yet had still been unsuccessful. It was hard to avoid the thought that his wheelchair had something to do with his inability to secure employment. He had a First Class honours degree in Construction Engineering and Management. Did that not mean anything?

His parents, grandfather and Christian friends kept trying to tell him not to worry for they were confident that 'the Lord had something' for him. They said that as though they really believed it but they too were probably growing anxious about Craig, who was becoming increasingly frustrated. Everyone kept saying that it was out of his hands and to leave it to the Lord. This was what he kept trying to do, dull winter day after dull winter day, but it was hard.

Eventually in February 2006 Craig was appointed as a consultant engineer with White, Young, Green, an English company that was expanding its operations in Northern Ireland. He was so grateful to God that He had, as so many had predicted, a plan for him, and soon settled into his new position as a project manager with the company.

For more than a year after that Craig continued in his employment, trained and played with the Gaelic Warriors and shared his faith with mostly youth audiences. These speaking engagements included special events such as a large Christian Endeavour Rally one Saturday night in Portadown and a Soul Café outreach programme in Ballymoney. On different other nights he spoke to groups of young people in Dromore Cathedral and Great Victoria Street Baptist Church.

As he continued to attend these different meetings Craig became more and more convinced that he had been prepared by God to fulfil a special dual role. The first of these was in what appeared to be a social capacity, that of encouraging disabled and wheelchair-bound people that a full life was possible, and would be essentially what they made it, whatever their situation. The other was to tell audiences, many of whom came to hear Craig because he was in a wheelchair when they wouldn't have been interested in him had he been able to stand or walk, that the Christian faith was real, and relevant to all the ups and downs of life.

One of the largest meetings he had addressed for some time was held in Newtownbreda Baptist Church, on the outskirts of Belfast on Easter Sunday, 8 April 2007. The theme of the service, based on the resurrection, was hope, and Craig was interviewed about his accident and where he had come to, through all the hospital, rehab and student experiences, from where he had been.

The message he had to convey was one of hope. He didn't hide the fact that there had been many dark days but then he contrasted that with the gloom of that band of faithful followers, both men and women, whose world had been turned upside down when Jesus was crucified. The outlook had been bleak for them, but when their Lord and Master rose from the dead joy in the present and hope for the future filled every heart.

Craig pointed out that the Christian faith was unique for its central figure was a Saviour who had died, but had risen from the dead and is alive for evermore. When the interviewer asked him about the 'tough times' he had been through he admitted that he had 'been through quite a bit,' particularly in the days directly after his accident. He went on immediately to focus the attention away from himself by declaring that this was nothing compared with what Jesus had suffered for him.

With the next European Wheelchair Rugby Championships scheduled for early June 2007 Craig became a lot busier. He hadn't been in full-time employment when he had first played for Ireland in the previous championship, but now he had to fit in training sessions after work. This meant trips to Dublin at least once during the week and over every weekend. Craig was keen to play his part in trying to improve the team's performance in the coming competition and so in addition to squad sessions he devised his own personal training routine, which he followed at home.

The training in Dublin was the most rigorous Craig had ever experienced and yet he knew that it was necessary if the Irish team was to make any kind of impact in the championships. This meant that when it came to June the party of players and assistants flew out to Finland feeling better prepared that they had done two years before.

It was a particular pleasure for Craig to have his dad, John, with him on the trip. He had attended most of the pre-tournament training sessions with his son, and had become involved in team management. John was one of a group who had assumed responsibility for the maintenance of the team's sporting wheelchairs. This could be quite a demanding task for the chairs took terrible hammerings during the matches!

When twelve national teams from all over Europe converged on Helsinki the Finnish capital had never seen so many wheelchairs together within its boundaries before. There was a carnival atmosphere about the entire event and as Craig felt more confident both in playing the game and with the organisation of the championships he was in a much better position to enjoy it all.

A disciplined training routine and a succession of bruising encounters with the Gaelic Warriors had made him a much more accomplished player than he had been in his first European Championships. He was proud to wear the Ireland shirt once more, this time as an experienced player, and looked forward to the first match, which was again against Great Britain.

The result was the same as last time, too. They were beaten by a substantial margin. This was disappointing, though generally predicted, against the reigning two-time champions but it in no way dampened Craig's passion for the game and he had an exciting, active and physically challenging time at the championships.

Although the Irish team had prepared a lot more thoroughly for these championships they were just a little piqued to discover that most of the other teams had done the same! The standard of play had risen so much, that although the games were tougher and faster than they had been in 2005 the results followed a familiar pattern. Ireland were again to finish in the bottom half of the league.

In the post championship analysis and briefing the Irish team coach complimented the performance of his players, considering that they were the only totally amateur team in the competition. He did, however, go on to remark that they would have to step up their professionalism and commitment to the sport if they were to improve their final placing significantly in 2009.

During the summer of 2007 Craig was approached by the Republic of Ireland television company, RTE. They were interested in doing a programme on wheelchair rugby and wanted to know if he would be willing to feature in it

As far as he was concerned there was no problem and a camera crew followed him to a training period with the Irish team. Their next stop was his home in Ballyclare, where mum, dad and sister Emma were asked to reflect on the past trauma of Craig's injury and his present involvement with wheelchair rugby.

When Craig was interviewed he came across as an inspiration. He said that he just wanted to get on with life despite his condition and when he first saw wheelchair rugby being played he determined to 'get into it.' There had been adjustments to be made to his lifestyle but his resolve saw him through and he had reached the very top in the sport. It had been his teenage dream to represent his country at rugby, and he had fulfilled his ambition, in a variant of the game.

Emma's admiration for her brother was very evident when she spoke and John was shown in his support role as wheelchair mechanic and general encourager. It was a comment made by his mum, however, mum whose prayers Craig had craved at his crisis point, that summed up the present situation for the family.

She was speaking of the great relationship that had always existed between Craig and his dad, from they had played games and discussed results and tactics together back before Craig had his accident. This had carried on to the present day in a different sporting discipline. They would, she recounted, come back from a game with the Gaelic Warriors or a championship series and spend the greater part of an evening discussing it all. It would be about who played well, or who 'didn't have his best game, 'or what modifications they could make to the chair, or how they could improve as a team.

"It is just like it used to be," she commented.

# Going for it ...
## in the heat

# Kerri's
## Story

# 1

# The Big Issue

IT LOOKED LIKE a typical playground scene during the morning break on a crisp day in early November. The pupils from Edenderry Primary School in Banbridge, Co. Down seemed determined to make the most of their short break from lessons despite a noticeable autumnal chill in the air.

Boys ran frantically after a football wherever it just happened to be kicked, but the girls were different. A few of them had a skipping rope in a corner, some of the younger ones were chasing each other around without either obvious pattern or reason, but most of the older girls were standing about in what they reckoned would be a 'ball-free' zone, just talking.

The duty teacher who was keeping a watchful eye on all the playground proceedings would have noticed four Primary 7 girls making their way from the senior to the junior playground. They were probably doing this in the hope of encountering fewer disturbances if they wanted to have a friendly chinwag. As they perched themselves on the long low windowsill of Miss Tate's classroom that was obviously what they were intending to do.

A closer observation would have revealed, however, that this wasn't just another meaningless girlish gabble about anything and everything. It was more organised than that. Rebecca McVeigh, who seemed to be doing most of the talking, had created a curiosity in the minds of three of her friends by telling them that she had something very important to share with them at break-time. That had left the trio to endure almost two hours of suspense, with just a slight inclination as to what it may be about.

The mystery unravelled when they noticed that Rebecca had brought what appeared to be a pretty well-worn Bible out with her and was holding it in her left hand. This was odd and left the other girls feeling a bit embarrassed. A Bible! That boring, uncool, old-fashioned book. What was Rebecca thinking of? Was she not embarrassed to be sitting there holding it? This was unheard of!

It soon became clear that it meant a lot to Rebecca and she wasn't embarrassed at all. The eleven-year old started the sharing of her 'secret' by informing her specially invited audience that what she was about to tell them was 'the best news they would ever hear in their lives.' And as if that weren't enough, it could lead them to making a very important choice.'

Her three friends looked slightly bewildered. What was she 'going on about?' 'The best news they had ever heard in their lives?' They had heard lots of wonderful things already. After all they were eleven years old and the senior pupils in school! What had they missed?

As curiosity rose even further following these opening remarks Rebecca studiously avoided the quizzical looks on the faces of her three friends. She was too busy opening the N.I.V. Bible with the Sellotaped spine at a page she had obviously selected for the occasion.

"It will make it easier for me to explain what it is I want to tell you if I read you a little bit or two out of the Bible first," she began.

This 'wasn't for' a couple of the girls Rebecca had led round to the junior playground where they could 'hopefully get a bit of peace and quiet.' They simply rose and ran back to join the rest of their classmates.

One stayed, though. She wasn't awfully sure why she stayed, but she did. It was probably partly because she didn't want to offend Rebecca, and she didn't think it very polite of the others to run off before even hearing what she wanted to say. It was also partly because there was something more to it than that. The prospect of hearing 'the best news of her life' had a mysterious appeal to it, and what was this 'important choice.' Who, for example, was expected to make it, and why, and when?

With her audience depleted by two-thirds Rebecca overcame her slight disappointment by adopting a more personal and casual approach. It left her free to share, on a one-to-one basis, with her classmate Kerri Shields.

"I'm sorry those other two have gone, but can I read to you anyway, Kerri?" she enquired.

"Sure, no problem," was Kerri's 'playing it cool' yet inquisitive response. If a few 'bits from the Bible' had something to do with this 'good news' she reckoned she might as well hear them.

Kerri glanced across as Rebecca began to read and noticed that the words she was reading had been underlined in red in her Bible. They must have been of very special significance. It struck her that Rebecca must have been 'doing work' on this Bible. She must spend a lot of time reading, marking and underlining it. Had she not enough homework to do that she needed to study the Bible as well?

When she had read out three or four short snippets from various carefully marked places Rebecca kept her Bible open and then began to explain the meaning of them. When all put together the gist of it was that God created everybody in the world but people don't want anything to do with Him. They would rather do life their own way. This is because they have sin in them. In spite of this rejection God loved all these people so much that He sent His son, Jesus, down to earth to die and take away their sins, so that they can get back in touch with Him again.

This was all fascinating stuff and there were so many things that Kerri's agile mind wanted to know. The first of them was why she had never heard of this before. She had been to church and knew there was a God and a man called Jesus. But the fact that they were mixed up together somehow and had any significance for her life was completely new to her.

Then there was this question about 'sin.' Surely everybody does wrong things in their lives, some worse than others, but then there's nobody perfect, is there? And how could God hold it against me? I try my best.

And how could Jesus dying on a cross make any difference to anything? Or why would He even want to die in the first place? The concept of the crucifixion of Jesus being anything more than a gruesome killing in olden day times in which a famous wise man was executed intrigued Kerri. She had heard about Jesus and His miracles and parables in Sunday School. She had sung 'Away in a Manger' at Christmas and 'Christ the Lord is risen today!' at Easter. But was there more to Jesus than that?

According to Rebecca, who sounded as though she actually knew Him personally, there was, and that was 'the good news!'

The conversation continued with Kerri asking question after question about who Jesus was and why He had come to earth, and her friend answering them one by one as they came.

At one stage Kerri looked past Rebecca at the others all 'doing their own thing' and wondered, 'what am I doing sitting here?' She had no answer to that except that she had become totally captivated by Rebecca's 'good news' explanations and her enthusiasm.

As part of this 'sharing' process Rebecca told Kerri that she was 'very special to God.' He had created her for Himself and that was why Jesus died for her. He wanted her to come to Him and get to know Him as a friend. If she believed Jesus died for her sins and prayed this to Him, they could be friends and meet one day in heaven. She would become a Christian.

Here was something new again. It had all suddenly turned very personal. Jesus wanted her, Kerri Shields, to pray to Him and He wanted to become friends with her.

How could she, though? How did she go about it? Where was He and how did she get to Him? Was this whole idea not completely mad? Was He not the creator of the world?

It was all so much to try and understand in one ten minute chat that it never even crossed Kerri's mind to make any sort of 'important choice' or personal commitment at that point. The simple sincerity of Rebecca's faith and her evident desire to share it with her friends made a profound impression on her, however.

It was definitely a big issue with her.

What Kerri couldn't understand was why it had left her with a feeling that she wanted to learn more about this. Why did she sense that Rebecca's 'something important' was actually something important? It had an intriguing ring of truth about it.

Could Rebecca's big issue ever become a big issue with her, too?

During the spring, and then on into the summer term in their final year at Primary School, the two classmates walked home together. As they came to know one another better during those days Kerri discovered that Rebecca was different, in a strangely attractive way, to any of the friends she had ever known up until then. She would give Kerri little booklets about Jesus and the Christian faith every now and again and these were always read with a mild but mounting curiosity.

When September came and both girls transferred into Form 1 in Banbridge Academy they found that they were in separate classes within the year group. This meant they did not see each other so often but it did not stop Rebecca taking the opportunity to invite Kerri along to special youth events in the church which she attended with her family, Ballydown Presbyterian.

It was during their second year in the Academy that Rebecca asked Kerri along to a special youth weekend in the church. This had been advertised as an 'Inside Out Weekend,' the aim probably being to encourage young people to accept Jesus into their lives and then share their Christian faith outwardly day by day.

Kerri agreed to go along to the Friday night rally and found it most impressive on two counts. Firstly she found that many of the young people there were like Rebecca. They had an appealing settled peace about them, a confidence coupled with an unmistakeable zest for life. The other aspect of the opening meeting of the weekend, which left a lasting impact on the thirteen-year-old, was the talk given by a man who had obviously lots of experience in speaking to teenagers.

He held everyone's attention as he described how young people could have their lives transformed by trusting in Christ. He said that Jesus had come to earth to live and die and rise again so that all who know Him should 'live life to the full.'

After the meeting, Rebecca, who thought Kerri seemed quite interested in what the speaker had been saying, asked her, "Would you like to become a Christian, Kerri? Would you like to say the prayer?'"

'The prayer' Rebecca was talking about turned out to be some words on the back of a little booklet, and was designed to help people articulate their desire to come to know Christ and make Him the 'ruler of their lives.' Kerri replied that she would 'like time to think about it' and if she wanted to say the prayer she would do it when she got home, by herself.

She may have only said that to please Rebecca or get out of making the decision but something kept the issue at the forefront of her mind. There was no escaping it. This was something she knew she should do; it seemed right. Kerri had been intrigued with this 'good news' of 'life to the full' since Rebecca had first explained it to her about two years ago. The time to make that 'important choice' had come.

Before getting into her bed that night Kerri sat on it and said 'the prayer.' This was not just a repetition of words, however. It represented the sincere commitment of a teenage heart. She began by thanking God for sending Jesus into the world to take away her sins, saying sorry for ignoring Him and then asking Him to come into her life. This was followed by a simple plea for help to follow Him wherever He may lead her in life from then on. She wanted to do it God's way. Then, suddenly afraid that she hadn't somehow 'done it right' or 'said exactly the right words' she read the prayer over again, word by word, from the back of the booklet.

Although she didn't feel any dramatic change come over her at that moment Kerri settled down to sleep in ten or fifteen minutes, satisfied. She had wanted to come to God, she had done it, and now she could sleep. That was it.

On Monday morning at break time Rebecca came looking for her friend. "Well, Kerri, how did it go on Friday night?" she enquired.

"I said the prayer before I went to sleep," came the shy, almost apologetic reply. "I'm not sure if it worked, but I meant it."

Kerri could in no way have anticipated the joy this simple confession of faith would generate in Rebecca. She began jumping up and down with excitement, squealing as she did so, "That's great, Kerri! Oh, that's wonderful! That's an answer to my prayers!"

The new convert was a little embarrassed and more than a little baffled at this spontaneous exuberance. "Calm down, Rebecca," she urged. "Surely it's not all that big a deal!" She realised, though, even as she was trying to curb her friend's instant outburst that she had done the right thing. It felt good now.

"Oh it is! It is!" Rebecca refused to be hushed. "It's the biggest deal of your life! You will soon find that out!"

The couple chatted animatedly right through until it was time to return to class, with each of them realising instinctively that a new, warm, God-inspired relationship now existed between them. When they parted at the bell Kerri couldn't help but think, as she had done back in Primary 7, of how big an issue Rebecca's Christian faith was in her life. It seemed to influence what she did, what she said, and even how she thought! Will it be like that with me? she wondered, casually.

It was around the same time that Kerri made the spiritual discovery of her life, that her sporting prowess, particularly as a squash player, was discovered. She had gone along to an after-school squash club with some friends. This club was run by Syd Moore, the squash coach in Banbridge and he spotted her potential. He asked her if she would like to join some others for extra coaching. Kerri was pleased to be recognised, took the coach up on his offer and it wasn't long until she had been identified as an up-and-coming talent in the sport. Within a year she had been selected as a member of the under-14 team representing Ireland at the home internationals against England, Scotland and Wales.

This gave Kerri an opportunity to shine in the sporting world and she also seemed to perform consistently well in her studies. She was conscious, however, that although she had made a Christian commitment, she was making little or no progress in that regard. Her faith hadn't become the big issue in her life that it should.

It just happened one day that she was talking to two girls in her class, Claire and Vicky, both of whom were Christians. When the discussion came around to their daily Bible reading, these two friends were surprised to learn that Kerri didn't even possess a 'youth' Bible of her own, one that she could study and mark like she had seen Rebecca doing.

That was a situation that needed remedied, Claire and Vicky decided. Setting out on the Christian life without a Bible was like starting out on a long car journey over unfamiliar roads without a map, they reckoned.

Later that week after school Vicky walked up with Kerri to a little Christian bookshop in the town and there, as a fourteen year-old, she bought her first Bible – a New Century Version Youth Bible. Then, when she brought it home she backed it in thick, embossed, orange wallpaper. She kept telling herself that she wanted to keep it clean and protected, as it was a paperback. That was true, but it also helped disguise it so that no one had to know about the compelling desire she had to read the Bible and learn more about Jesus. It was so comforting to read little bits of it with the help of the 'youth notes ' inside it, every night. Then she talked to God in prayer, asking Him to carry her through the next day.

As she progressed through her Grammar school career Kerri excelled at sport. She went on to represent Ulster and Ireland in squash at Under-16, and Under19 level, attending squad sessions both in Belfast and Dublin and tournaments all over the British Isles and Europe. Kerri also played twice for Ireland in the European Junior Championships and once in the World Junior Championships. In addition to her squash commitments she was playing hockey for the 1st XI during her last three years at grammar school. By the time it came to her final year at the school Kerri was selected as Head Girl of Banbridge Academy.

What, though, of her Christian faith? As she became more taken up with her sport, her studies and an active social life God became relegated to the background.

It was useful to know Him and to have Him to call upon in frantic prayer in a tight spot. There were a number of 'Oh please God help me win this match,' type prayers in squash tournaments or, 'Please help me God to remember all the stuff I need to pass this exam,' panic petitions before GCSE or A-level exams for which she felt ill-prepared.

There were so many things going on in her life that living and witnessing for Christ had been pushed far down her list of priorities. It hadn't yet become her big issue.

Would it ever?

# 2

# Why Do I Just Want to Cry?

HAVING ACHIEVED THE expected results in her A-level examinations Kerri was accepted to study engineering at Keble College, Oxford University. This proved to be quite a shock to the system in many ways. She was away from home and without the constant daily support of her mum and dad. Her elder brother Martin was already at Oxford. That was one bonus. The subject was much more difficult than anything she had ever encountered before and the method of study completely different. People didn't seem to understand her accent, and although she was one of thousands of students in the famous university city, she felt strangely isolated.

When Kerri came home for Christmas she didn't want to go back. Her mum persuaded her to give it another try, at least for the next term, and if that didn't work out then they could investigate other options. There were only two shafts of light on what Kerri had considered a very dark horizon, and it was these that made her decide to go back and give Oxford another go.

One of these concerned sport, the other study. Although she had only been there one term Kerri had already become recognised as number one lady in the Oxford University Squash team. If she were to give up she would lose her place, not to mention her Oxford Sporting 'Blue,' which she would be awarded after playing against Cambridge University in the varsity match in February. When she struggled with her studies in what had been perceived for years as a male-dominated discipline, Kerri had been helped by Ash, her tutorial partner. Ash, who had come up from Eton, was very capable and kind and would encourage her when he saw her having problems, with, "Don't worry, Kerri. All you have to do is read this – or do that." If Ash was going to be there, and he was, she'd give it a go..

Second term proved to be a little better for that was when Kerri met Abi, another first year student. As the two girls became more friendly and Kerri had someone who understood her and shared her passion for sport she felt less homesick. She also began playing a wider variety of sports and so before finishing her second term to return to Banbridge at Easter she had played hockey for the University second XI and represented her College, Keble, at netball, basketball and football as well as squash and hockey.

During her Easter vacation Kerri's mum had suggested that she should enter the Miss Northern Ireland competition and she had been invited by a friend to attend a heat in Magherafelt. Kerri, as a modest young lady was rather flattered, and not one to turn down a new experience, decided to go along. Before that day was out she had been selected for the finals, which were to be held in Belfast in June!

When she returned to Oxford to complete her first year, Kerri found that it was close season for most of the sports she had been playing during the winter and spring terms and so she tried her hand at some rowing. The final eight week term saw Kerri spending the first four of them rowing, training to compete in the 'Summer Eights' rowing regatta. When the regatta was over Kerri knew what loomed over her. First year engineering students at Oxford must sit and pass four examinations, called prelims, before being admitted into their second year.

After four weeks of trying to brush up on a whole year of University work Kerri felt rather under-prepared to sit these exams, one a day for four days, Wednesday to Saturday. An added complication was that her last exam was on Saturday 9 June, which was the date the Miss Northern Ireland Competition weekend was scheduled to begin in the Europa Hotel, Belfast.

Having completed three grilling exams, Kerri finally made it to the last one. She rushed through it, dashed out avoiding all the champagne spraying and other celebrations, was driven to Heathrow Airport and caught a plane to Belfast. The plan was that she should go straight to the Europa Hotel to join the other girls, but her bags didn't come through. She couldn't believe it! So she went home instead and on

Sunday morning Kerri found it funny sitting with the other contestants having her hair done for the Miss Northern Ireland contest in clothes that she hadn't even considered good enough to take with her to university!

The final judging session for the competition took place on Monday evening 11 June 2001, and Kerri finished third. It had been a really 'different' experience, one that Kerri simply appreciated being part of, and so 'a podium finish' was an added bonus.

A few weeks later, Kerri was made aware that it hadn't been a good idea to rush through her final paper, for although it was what had been her best subject all year, she failed that exam. She was required to re-sit it in August and after doing some intensive study, with the spectre of 'what happens if I fail this?' lingering over her head, she passed it with distinction.

With the prelims now all behind her, Kerri thought she would really enjoy her second year at Oxford. There were no exams at the end of that year so she could play a lot of sport, do a little work, and generally have fun. She still loved her squash and had been selected as Oxford University women's squash captain as well as playing for the Ulster senior ladies team that won the inter-county championships.

What Kerri couldn't understand as that second year progressed, however, was that no matter how many successes she tried to total up, there was always a sense that she ought to be feeling much happier, much more at peace with herself, than she did. There was something else elusive out there that she couldn't quite identify, and so couldn't quite grasp.

Why did this attractive, intelligent, multi-talented student at Oxford University feel so unsatisfied half the time?

Why did this popular socialite who had hockey pals, posh pals, funny pals, serious pals, rich pals and any other desirable kind of pals she would ever need, feel lonely half the time?

Why did this young woman who had endless intellectual challenges to fill her head and ceaseless activity, both sporting and practical, to fill her hands, feel that there was a huge and bottomless hole in her heart?

Why did she feel like crying half the time?

Although she hadn't been living as a Christian, or reading her Bible as regularly as she had done in past times, a thought crossed Kerri's mind that perhaps there was something more to life than she saw in front of her. This led her to pray desperately at times, "God is there not more to life than this? I am bored with all this, sick of all the humdrum and activities of life. Am I missing something? What should I be doing?"

In an attempt to find that 'something more,' Kerri went down to St. Aldate's, a nearby Church of England, a couple of Sunday mornings, when not away at a squash tournament elsewhere. She would slip in, listen, and often try to slip out again without becoming involved, but as she did so she was challenged that perhaps the answer to her emptiness lay in what was here and what these people had. Everyone seemed so content, so satisfied with life and so happy to be with each other.

Unknown to Kerri, a friend from College had noticed her at church and decided to follow up what she assumed to be a sign of some sort of faith with an invitation. Kerri had gone to a Monday evening 'black-tie dinner' in Keble College and was chatting afterwards in the college bar when her friend came across to her and said, "I saw you at St. Aldate's one Sunday morning a week or two ago, Kerri, and I know that you are into all kinds of sport. There is a group called 'Christians in Sport' that meet every Tuesday morning at 8 o'clock down in Trinity College. I was wondering if you would like to go along? I will call for you tomorrow morning if you like."

"Yes, I suppose I could make it," Kerri replied after a few seconds thought. She was slightly hesitant only because she wondered if she could make it for 7.45 a.m. the morning after a 'night out.'

Her friend promised to call for her in the morning and when she arrived at Kerri's door, Kerri was ready to go. The title 'Christians in Sport' had intrigued her. Anything 'in Sport' would have appealed to her.

Kerri hadn't been long in that early morning meeting until she realised that there was something about it, and particularly the people at it, that struck a chord with her. The guys and girls there were from different colleges and she already recognised a few of them through her sporting connections. Though coming from a variety of backgrounds, when together that morning they all seemed to share a common denominator. It was their faith. Most of them appeared to have Bibles with them for a start, and seemed very keen to open them. Someone gave a short talk on a Bible theme and then the large group divided into smaller groups to 'pray for their team mates.'

To the others it was a normal Tuesday morning Prayer and Bible study group, but to Kerri Shields, there on her first visit, it was a shock. She was on the verge of tears again. Why does this make me want to cry? she wondered.

She knew the answer instinctively. The Bible reading and prayer had touched her soul. Deep down she realised that it made sense. Life does have meaning, there is a reason for it all. This was the 'more' she had been missing; the life that was worth being bothered about. The tears she was trying to hold back were not of despair and disillusionment as before, but of discovery and revelation.

This was real! These people's trust in God was simple and sincere but yet deep, solid and profound, all at the same time! It was real to them, personal and life influencing, and Kerri wanted it also. They reminded her of Rebecca and her enthusiasm for her Bible. The whole meeting took her back in thought to the night in her bedroom when she had, as a thirteen-year old, said a prayer committing her life to Jesus.

Kerri went to the Christians in Sport meeting the next Tuesday morning, and the next. It had given her a new focus in life. She unearthed her Bible and began to study it again with some of the other students at different times during the week. It seemed so meaningful now and so often it spoke right into her situation. She just couldn't read enough of it.

This revival of something in Kerri which had been in hibernation for most of her teenage years, led her to attend St. Aldate's church every Sunday she was free. There she met Simon Ponsonby, the student minister, who had the job of pastoring and organising the University students who came along to church. Before long he and a friend from Christians in Sport, had encouraged her to attend other midweek student activities in the church as well.

It was great. Kerri was beginning to understand life, beginning to discover its true meaning, beginning to learn what was worth bothering with and what wasn't. This was the kind of 'life to the full' that Jesus had talked about when He was on earth.

Kerri's third year at Oxford began with her having to ask permission from her tutors to take the first three days off university lectures and classes. She had been selected to play for Ireland on the Senior Ladies squash team in the World Championships in Denmark in early October 2002. This was a particular thrill for it was another step up for Kerri in her squash career and it gave her the opportunity to meet, and compete against, some of the top lady players in the world. She counted it an honour to represent her country in her favourite sport but something else was also happening with her squash. As God had been changing her understanding of life, Kerri was gradually realising that He could also change her attitude to sport. So far it had all been about how good she was, each match being the 'be all and end all,' with the outcome dictating her confidence in life in the days to follow. Now, though, Kerri was seeing that her talents on the squash court had in fact been given to her by God, and perhaps it should be a joyful pleasure to play her squash. Perhaps through giving her best on court she could please God and thus satisfy herself much more.

As that year went on at university and final examinations drew closer Kerri began to feel unsure of herself and very panicky. There was so much to learn, and know, before the end of June. Would she be able for it, or was she going to fall at the last hurdle? She needed the calming effect of personal contact with God in prayer and the prayerful support of her Christian friends.

Her 21st birthday celebration back at home in Banbridge in April 2003 was not the happy event that Kerri had hoped for. Worry for the looming 'finals' overshadowed the evening and she found it difficult to feel God's peace amongst it all,

On returning to the university city after the Easter recess, Kerri tried to work frantically to prepare for her examinations but the continued pressure made her even more upset. Every time she tried to concentrate on her studies, waves of panic set in and tears appeared. She was speaking to Simon Ponsonby one day after a church service and suddenly burst into tears. Recognising that Kerri was in a fragile emotional state Simon suggested that she ought to call round and see his wife, Tiffany, 'sometime soon.' "She's lovely, and she'll take care of you. She'll love to pray with you," he assured her.

Anxious to do anything, or meet anybody, that could help her, she took Simon up on his suggestion and called in to see Tiffany later that day. Kerri found it a tremendous boost to her flagging confidence to be able to talk through her concerns with someone who genuinely cared for her. As they discussed a variety of issues Tiffany constantly shared relevant bits out of the Bible and assured the nervous student that God could help her through every situation that would arise in her life, including the exams that were coming up.

With Tiff as a solid support now, one of Kerri's most difficult days was when Abi had finished her exams and she had yet to start. Kerri thought she would like to go down and help her friend celebrate but was only halfway there when she had to turn back. She ended up at Tiffany's door in floods of tears.

Kerri was welcomed inside and she was extremely touched when Simon and Tiffany's little five-year-old son asked his mum, "Please can I pray for Kerri too?"

When his mum had said he could he put his hand on Kerri's arm and prayed with complete sincerity, "God, please help Kerri and make her happy again." Kerri put her arm around his shoulder, and before she had got the words, "Thank you, Nat," out, tears of genuine gratitude were glistening down her cheeks. What love! What a blessing from God this family was to Kerri.

A mixture of peer pressure, inadequacy and fear had begun to shatter Kerri's emotions, with the only positive being the value of both individual and collective prayer, and the blessing various Bible studies she enjoyed with other Christian students were to her. God was often gracious enough to bring back to her mind a relevant verse, which she had heard in them and which comforted her in her troubles or guided her in her struggles.

A few weeks before her finals Kerri had a phone call from Rebecca. Through some kind of a contact between both sets of parents back in Banbridge, Rebecca, who was studying at Trinity College, Dublin, had learnt that Kerri was 'rather upset ' about her exams.' She was ringing to offer her support and prayed for Kerri over the phone. Again this was so comforting. Rebecca had made an international call just to show her friend some Christian love.

With the power of God and the support of such friends and family behind her why should Kerri feel the need to run away from the exams and the whole situation?

At the final hurdle now, Kerri's anguish heightened to such an extent that her mum came over and stayed with her. Mum had already offered endless hours of listening, encouragement, advice and support. She came to Oxford to spend a few days looking after all the practicalities of Kerri's life, leaving her free to do nothing but study, or at least try to study, amongst all the worry and fear.

En route to one of her exams Kerri was riding her bicycle down from her accommodation in Keble College to the examination halls. She was dressed in traditional Oxford undergraduate subfusc, with black bow at the neck of a white blouse, black skirt, and her gown billowing in the wind.

What a casual observer would not have noticed, however, was that she could barely see to steer the machine for her eyes were brimming full of tears. Nor could they be aware that the girl on the bike was praying as hard as she could.

"Oh God, please help me here today," she begged. "Help me to remember some things so I can complete this paper. I just want to get through this! Please, God. Please…"

God heard and answered her prayers, and the prayers of others for her too. When it came to the remainder of the exams she was convinced that He was, indeed, with her. It was not an easy time but verses which comforted Kerri a lot throughout this period were 2 Corinthians 12; 9-10. These helped her to appreciate that human weakness provides the ideal opportunity for the display of divine power. And if ever she needed the mighty power of God in her life it was now, for she felt completely inadequate.

The results were posted later in the summer and one of the names on the notice board was Kerri Shields. She had graduated with Second Class honours, Second division.

Kerri, who had asked herself dozens of times during her three years at Oxford, 'Why am I crying?' was at it again.

This time, though, her tears were of absolute joy and delight and relief.

But was that her crying finished now, for good?

# 3

# Shining Out The Other Side

KERRI STILL HAD another year to do at Oxford to complete her Master of Engineering degree. This should be a much less pressurised experience since 60% of the year was based on a project dissertation for which Kerri had put forward her own suggested topic.. She wanted something in which she would be really interested, so what better than squash? Combining her love of the game with the need to study engineering she opted to design a 'Deployable Championship Squash Court' with four glass walls used for arena audiences.

She set to work on this with a will and with less formal lectures to attend she was able to organise her own time. This left her free to attend most of the prayer and Bible study sessions with Christians in Sport, and more activities in St. Aldate's.

Simon and others in leadership in the Church appreciated Kerri's commitment and so were grateful when she offered to help teach in the Sunday School. This was to prove a great time of combining systematic Bible study with real life challenges from inquisitive teenage minds. She also began attending the CCC mornings, coffee, croissants and communion, every Wednesday from 7.45 until 8.45 a.m. Thursday evening was 'Risky Living' time for students in the church. This was a dinner followed by a time of singing and then Bible teaching, which was aimed at challenging young Christians to live effectively for Christ.

When Kerri witnessed a baptismal service in St. Aldate's one Sunday evening in November she was gripped with a sense of longing. A number of young people gave a personal testimony to their faith in Christ and then were baptised by immersion. Each baptism brought with it a look of joy and delight on the face of the person being baptised and created an almost infectious atmosphere of rejoicing throughout the entire congregation.

One of the men leading the service had earlier explained the significance of baptism by immersion for those not familiar with its practical and present day relevance. He said that Jesus had been baptised by John, and that the Bible taught that being baptised was a very practical way of being publicly identified with Christ. It was an acknowledgement that Jesus had taken the punishment that we rightly deserved for our sin. He had also given us new life, we belonged to Him and the life we were now living for Him was fulfilling and right.

As the service proceeded, Kerri determined to be baptised. I want to do that! she decided. She had matured a lot in her faith through all the ups and downs of the previous year and a half and now knew how right, real and forever her relationship with Jesus was set to be. 'I guess others can know now also,' she reckoned.

A few days later, when speaking to Simon Ponsonby, she asked him to let her know when the next baptismal service was coming up in the church for she was keen to be baptised. He assured her he would.

During the Christmas vacation Kerri was browsing in the Christian bookshop where she had bought her first Bible and picked up a book with the rather startling title, 'The Cross and The Switchblade.' When she looked at it she discovered that the book beside it was called 'Run Baby Run,' and was by the same author. The titles and blurb on the back covers left her wanting to learn more about them and so she bought them both.

Kerri began reading these books and found them interesting, challenging and inspirational in a grim and gripping kind of way. They were about the power of God to transform the lives of teenagers who had become caught up in the violent underworld of gang-related crime in New York. She was also intrigued to learn that Teen Challenge, the group that David Wilkerson had founded, initially to help reach out to these teenagers, had now grown into a worldwide Christian organisation. It would be good, she thought, to find out more about Teen Challenge sometime

When she returned to her studies and to St. Aldate's Kerri was speaking to Simon one day and told him about these two 'fantastic' books she had bought. She had, she said, finished the first one and was on to the second, and although they were both 'rough in parts' she had found them spellbinding. Simon told her that 'The Cross and the Switchblade' was one of the first books he had read after having given his life to Jesus, and it had a tremendous influence on his attitude to Christian living and outreach.

Just before Kerri left Oxford to come back to Northern Ireland for Easter Simon told her that another baptismal service was being planned for May and asked her if she was still interested. She replied that reflection during the intervening period had left her even more convinced than ever that she ought to be baptised. Yes, she would like to be included. On confirming that she was more committed than ever to being baptised Simon told her that there would be a couple of preparation classes before the baptismal service and he would let her know the dates later.

That term had been busy with putting the finishing touches to her project and playing squash as well as her increasing involvement with church and Christians in Sport. Kerri was captain of the Oxford University women's squash team again and president of 'Atalantas,' the University Women's Sporting Blues society that helped the University's sportswomen, financially and in other ways, to achieve their potential in the sporting arena.

More diligent studying of her Bible and the reading of those two books led her to feel a growing desire to do something for God by devoting some of her time and energy to Him. She was due to graduate finally in the summer. What could she do, or where should she go, after that?

There was a sale on in the little Christian bookshop in Banbridge over the Easter period and a few days before she was due to return to England Kerri was in browsing again. She had developed a tremendous craving for Christian literature and was looking for something to read on the plane on the way back. There were so many books to choose from, but eventually she picked one from a shelf and when she read phrases like 'tell tale signs of drug addiction,' 'apprehended by the police' and 'rescued from a foundering fishing boat,' on the back cover, she decided that it would probably be a good story, and bought it.

The first time she had a spare minute between playing squash and visiting and phoning friends, she brought out, and began to read, her new book. This was entitled 'Out of The Deep' and was by an author she had never heard of called Noel Davidson. It was about a family in Scotland. The parents were Christians but their three sons had become heroin addicts. There were so many issues involved in it. The parent's dilemma, the sons' rebellion, God's ultimate provision. Kerri found it compelling. She was finishing it in Belfast City airport waiting for her flight back to Heathrow and was sitting in the lounge holding back the tears.

It wasn't just the story that had affected her but when she came to the part in the story where the lads went to rehab in Teen Challenge she could barely believe it. So Teen Challenge was in Britain. David Wilkerson's books had made her determined to find out more about Teen Challenge when she had completed her studies. 'Out of The Deep' had merely confirmed this conviction for her. This, like baptism, was something that must go on her 'To Do List,' straightaway.

April was an eventful month, for Kerri was busily engaged preparing her project for assessment and studying for final examinations. There was a big change from the year before, however. Kerri had become more stable in her Christian faith and had come to rely more on God to lead and guide her through all the aspects of life. This was a relief to her parents who had been desperately worried about her at the end of third year.

There were to be two baptismal preparation sessions before the service, which had been arranged for Sunday 30 May. These were held in early and mid-May and amongst the matters raised and discussed at them was the fact that each candidate for baptism would be expected to give a short explanation about how they had come to faith in Christ, and why they wanted to be baptised. They were to do this just before entering the water.

As Kerri sat with a sheet of paper in front of her to jot down what it was she wanted to say she found it very difficult. Her problem was that she wanted to be strong in making a public declaration of her faith but didn't want to make her family think she was weird or she had become caught up in some cult. She had invited her mum and dad, her sister and two brothers to come to the service but she wasn't sure who could make it.

When Kerri rose from the desk her head was in a whirl, her heart was tearing itself in two and the paper was still blank. Why am I doing this? she asked herself. Do I really have to 'go public' with my commitment? What difference is it going to make in the long run?

On Sunday 23 May, just a week before she was due to be baptised, Kerri was coming out of the room where she had been teaching her Sunday School class and met Tiffany face to face. She took one look at the friend who had been so good and patient with her through so many trying times, and started to sob.

"What's wrong, Kerri?" Tiffany asked at once.

"I can't do it! I'm pulling out!" came the tearful response.

"Don't worry, we can help to pray with you through them in the same way as we did last year." Tiffany was trying to be most reassuring.

"It's not my exams I'm worried about, Tiff. It's my baptism!" Kerri exclaimed.

" What?! Well don't worry about that, either," the minister's wife, though surprised, was most understanding. "We can talk through whatever is worrying you, and pray about it," she went on to console.

Tiffany took time with Kerri on another occasion after that and as they prayed together she felt more at peace with the whole baptism event. She still couldn't decide how she was going to overcome her unease about declaring her Christian commitment in front of her family and friends.

Her reservations were dispelled when she went with some friends to a prayer evening in Birmingham the Wednesday before her baptism.. Kerri sat there, listening to prayer requests being announced and prayers being offered, but she seemed strangely detached from it all. She had her own very personal point for prayer and she chatted it through with God.

"God, please guide me as to what I should say at my baptism and bring along whoever You want. Help me to trust Your will to be done, not mine," was her request. As she prayed this way throughout the evening she was given an answer. It didn't come in any dramatic way, but just with a calm assurance in her head that helped heal the shakiness in her heart.

Kerri knew it was the right thing to do and she shouldn't be afraid of anything or anybody. She would trust God and go for it. Enjoy it even!

The remainder of the week was spent building up her confidence in that assurance and when Sunday arrived, and time for the baptismal service to begin, Kerri had her notes prepared and was up at the front with the rest.

There were eight people waiting to be baptised that evening and Kerri was to be number eight. This allowed her and the audience to become familiar with the procedure and by the time it came her turn to step forward she was unbelievably calm. She usually hated public speaking and often felt sick with nerves, but now in front of over 500 people she wasn't the slightest bit afraid! Many people who had been a part of her life, including her mum and dad and Rebecca who had read the Bible to her at school and prayed with her over the phone the previous year, were present and she was so thrilled that they had made the effort to come.

Kerri's testimony was clear, and honest. She told of her upbringing in Banbridge, saying the prayer of wanting to become a Christian at thirteen, years apart from God and that invitation to go along to Christians in Sport in Oxford. She then outlined her gradual realisation that she was a child of God and how her emotional and academic struggles had led her to reading the Bible more often and praying more meaningfully. This increased time with God had led her eventually to 'come shining out the other side of the great dark cloud' that had surrounded her during her exams and sometimes even in life. She was 'grounded now' as she was 'letting God work in me and in my life.'

'Shining out the other side' was no understatement, either. Her face was glowing as she went on to conclude her remarks by saying, "I want today to reaffirm my baptism vows and live with Jesus by my side."

With that she walked down the steps into the tank where Simon was waiting to baptise her. He lowered her into the water and when she stood up again the congregation began to sing, 'Great is Thy faithfulness, You never change, You never fail, O God.'

It was such a precious, triumphal moment for Kerri. The deep joyful smile seemed fixed on her face. She knew she had made the right choice.

On wiping the water from her eyes she was thrilled to discover that two very important women in her life were up by her side. They were her mum and Tiffany. Mum, who had stepped up out of her seat, ran to the front of the church and was crouching down beside the tank with her hand on her daughter's shoulder and Tiffany had her hand on her head. She was praying that God would bless her.

Light refreshments were available after the service and that was when Kerri brought the two ladies, who had come to her side at her baptism, together in less formal circumstances. Her introduction of, "Mum, this is Tiffany, Simon's wife," was sufficient to instigate a pleasant conversation between them all as they enjoyed their jam doughnuts. Later in the evening Kerri and her parents and friends went down to the local pub, 'The Head of The River,' to relax together over a drink and Charlie, the senior minister from St. Aldate's joined them. Kerri was pleased to see everyone together and so thankful that it had been such a wonderful day.

It had all been so real and when Kerri thanked her mum for coming and she replied with a reaction of mothers down the ages, "As long as you're happy I'm happy," she was full of praise to God. There could be no doubt about it. He had placed, and kept, His mighty hand on her, leading her gently to Him, and then guiding her gently through with Him, her four years at University.

When it came time for her final examinations Kerri's 'Deployable Championship Squash Court,' was well received and she completed her exams with a lot less turmoil than the previous year.

Kerri Shields, Master of Engineering, had come 'shining out the other side' of her troubles, her baptism and Keble College, Oxford.

Where was she going to 'shine' now though, in employment, and more importantly, for Jesus?

And what of her resolve to find out more about Teen Challenge?

# 4

# Teen Challenge

WITH THE CONVICTION that she should contact Teen Challenge and possibly even become involved with them in some way, having deepened within her during her last two terms at Oxford, Kerri decided to find out what she could about the organisation. From their website she sourced, amongst lots of other interesting information, the contact details for the Teen Challenge centre in south Wales. She rang the telephone number and after expressing a desire to learn more about the ministry of Teen Challenge was invited to 'come down to Wales and have a look around sometime.'

Having had her interest further aroused by the information she had gleaned through this initial contact, Kerri decided to respond to the suggestion, and arranged to go for a visit after she finished at university. She stayed overnight with a friend in Port Talbot and she and her mum drove Kerri across to the Teen Challenge Centre in Gorslas the following day.

In the course of the visit Kerri had an interview with Pastor John Ivanson, who was Principal of the Teen Challenge School of Ministry and he introduced her to some of the students currently following the course. She was then shown around Hope House where she met a number of the girls who were on the rehabilitation programme.

Jenny, one of the ladies on the administrative staff told Kerri that she had a spare room in her house and that she would be very welcome to come and stay with her if she decided to do the course. When leaving the centre Kerri felt this was right and that spending time there would give her a practical insight into what God was really like, and what He had done, and was still doing, in the lives of others.

Kerri then set off to travel in the Far East. She visited Thailand, Singapore and Bali before flying south to spend some time with an uncle in Melbourne. When she was there Lynn, one of her cousins, arrived out from the U.K. to join her.

On the day the two young women were leaving to travel to Sydney, Kerri's uncle Noel said, "I would like to become one of your sponsors for that Teen Challenge programme you were telling me about, Kerri. Will you let me know the details when you get home from your travels?" Kerri was delighted at this and took it as a further indication that she should go to Teen Challenge. She had been asked to raise a number of sponsors to help with the funding of her Teen Challenge course if she opted to do it. Uncle Noel was the first to volunteer.

Having spent a few nights in Sydney and visited the famous tourist attractions in the city the pair of cousins took a cheap internal flight to Brisbane. Their final destination was Cairns on Queensland's northeast coast and it was going to take a number of long coach trips to make it there with a few breaks in between.

The girls' next stop on their journey northwards was at a hostel in the resort of Mission Beach, and on the Sunday Kerri decided to try and find a church. She had hoped that she would be able to attend a church service every Sunday morning on her travels. On asking around at the hostel she was told that there was a church 'not very far away,' and was given directions. It was a warm September morning and Kerri was looking forward to walking there. The description of 'not very far away' proved misleading, however, for it took her almost an hour and a half to reach the church!

Kerri found the service most encouraging. The small country congregation, with an average age of about fifty, was so welcoming and interested in the young traveller. It was wonderful to meet people on the 'other side of the world' who also wanted to read the Bible and praise God. The first hymn that was sung thrilled her heart and sent her mind racing homewards. It was 'What a friend we have in Jesus,' which was written by Joseph Scriven who had been born in her hometown of Banbridge. It was also both her, and her cousin's, favourite hymn from church as kids. Kerri laughed to think that she had come all the way across the world to find people singing these well known words.

When the service was over there was tea and biscuits. Kerri ended up speaking to everyone there, all ten of them. One elderly lady enquired where she was staying. When Kerri told her that she was in the Youth Hostel she exclaimed at once, "I live right beside the Hostel. You walked here! I will give you a lift back in my car."

It was extremely kind of the lady to think of the young visitor and the short trip back turned out to be quite an experience. The car had seen many miles and appeared to Kerri to be falling apart and her driver seemed to imagine she was Thelma or Louise out of the film. She drove along at a leisurely pace, slumped in her seat like a 'surfer dude' with her elbow sticking out the window. With every window in the car rolled down as far as it could go because of the heat Kerri couldn't hear a word the lady was saying! When she did pick up a few words and try to make a sensible reply there was no response. The driver couldn't hear what she was saying either.

When she was left off at the Hostel Kerri thanked the lady for the lift and walked back in to meet Lynn with a little smile on her face and a contented glow in her heart. It had been an eventful morning, a morning to remember.

The cousins eventually arrived in Cairns for their last weekend in Australia and Kerri was delighted to discover that Hillsong were conducting a four-day Christian mission in the city. She missed the Friday night meeting and would be too late to find her way to the Saturday night one but determined that she would make it to the Sunday and Monday rallies if at all possible.

Lynn had become accustomed to Kerri looking out for a church to attend every Sunday and that was fine. She was a bit taken aback though when Kerri said she wanted to spend Monday night, their last night in Australia, at 'a church thing.' She wanted them to go out in Cairns together but Kerri didn't change her mind.

Although aware of her travelling companion's frustration Kerri still went to the Hillsong meeting. To her this was a blessing from God and an opportunity not to be missed, as it was so difficult to find Christian fellowship when travelling.

On leaving Australia the next morning the cousins spent some time touring New Zealand before returning to Northern Ireland. The decision that Kerri had then to make was whether or not to fully commit to doing the Teen Challenge course in January and if so how she would raise the funds.

Having thought and prayed it all through, and with Uncle Noel's initial pledge behind her she decided to go for it. To help raise the funds required for her upkeep on the programme Kerri immediately started looking for a job. She worked in a clothes shop in Banbridge before gaining two months engineering experience with Armstrong & Taylor, of Hillsborough. Kerri saved all the money she earned and it would be a help but it would not be enough to meet all her expenses and so she began approaching members of the family and some close friends asking them if they would like to sponsor her. In the course of explaining why she was looking for sponsorship Kerri was very pleased to be able to tell them about Teen Challenge, the School of Ministry, and her personal desire to develop her Christian faith.

Uncle Noel from Melbourne had been the first to pledge financial assistance to her in sponsorship and there were others to follow his lead, back in Northern Ireland. Kerri's dad was one of a large family and four of them, two brothers, Terry and Victor, and two sisters, Elizabeth and Gwen, were happy to sponsor their niece. Her mum's brother and sister, Robert and Sheila also declared themselves willing to help, as did others of the extended family circle. Great-aunt Elsie and her two daughters Maureen and Margaret were pleased to hear that Kerri was planning to go to the Teen Challenge School of Ministry and promised their support also. Even her friend from Swansea who had offered her accommodation gave her a donation, as did her home church in Banbridge.

It was gratifying to be so generously supported in her wish to spend some time seeing how God had changed the lives of so many people and learning what she could about Him through Bible study and new relationships. Kerri started out on the course enthusiastically yet slightly apprehensively. The Teen Challenge School of Ministry was a world apart from Keble College, Oxford. There her fellow-students had been the top performers in grammar schools from around the world. Her fellow-students here were largely people who had been converted to Christ, having spent at least part of their earlier lives in drink or drug addiction, something about which Kerri was totally naïve. The aim of studying at Oxford had been to obtain a degree and through that establish oneself in a career for life. The aim of the School of Ministry was to train people to study the Scriptures and share their personal faith with others in order to point them to the true meaning and purpose of life.

There were three basic elements to the course: life skills, Bible study and evangelism. Kerri was quite an accomplished young lady and life skills were no problem to her. She loved the Bible teaching sessions. It was a new experience for Kerri to study books in, and themes from, both the Old and New Testaments systematically. The unit on evangelism consisted of classroom teaching initially and then practical experience in the community later in the programme. Classes in the School of Ministry were from 8.00 a.m. until 1.00 p.m. each day and with the rest of the day free Kerri soon found a way to make a profitable use of her time. She took up an afternoon job with an international engineering firm, which had a local office in Swansea, and joined a racquets club where she could play squash in the evenings.

The practical element of the evangelism course allowed Kerri to work alongside other members of the group. Her first experience of this came when she accompanied Julie Murray, a senior leader in Hope House, and Pastor Jay Fallon from one of the local churches on to the streets of the nearby town of Ammanford on Friday mornings. Kerri admired Julie's and Jay's fearless yet courteous approach to the people, whether old or young, as they engaged them in conversation, telling them about Jesus and offering to pray with them if they wished. It took Kerri some time to feel comfortable talking to complete strangers on the street but as she relaxed she realised that there were actually people who were happy to chat and who wanted to hear about God.

Alison Kavanagh, one of the young women in the School of Ministry at the same time as Kerri, was on fire for God. Her life had been totally transformed after coming to Christ in her second day at Hope House as a hopeless drug addict. Now all Alison wanted to do was tell others about the Lord, and the mighty change He had brought about in her entire being, physically, mentally, emotionally and spiritually.

Just before Easter, Alison and Kerri were part of a team sharing an evangelistic mission in Newport, south Wales, Alison's hometown. The former heroin addict's enthusiasm was infectious. As they went out day by day to invite people to the evening services, Alison would say, "Come on, Kerri. We have to tell them. I want everybody in Newport to know about Jesus!" It was an exhilarating experience for Kerri to surf along on the high tide of 'Ali's' spiritual ardour.

Perhaps the most demanding of all the practical evangelism experiences for Kerri during that six-month period in Teen Challenge was towards the end of her term when she went to Glasgow to work with an outreach team.

She enjoyed the daytime element of the programme for this involved going into inner city schools to speak to classes of young people. One or two of the former addicts in the group would tell of the devastating effect that drugs had on their lives and then there would be a question and answer time. This was what Kerri liked. With her educational background she was well equipped to answer all kinds of questions about God and faith and the Christian life. Questions about drink and drugs she left to the other members of the panel. Kerri usually came away from the school visit sessions feeling that God had enabled her to help young lives and that was encouraging.

It was working out on the streets at night that she found more difficult. This was when the team set out in a specially equipped bus to tour the streets of the city in the late evenings. They had tea and coffee making facilities on board plus photographs and videos of addicts whose lives had been changed since conversion, and suitable Christian literature. The aim was to tell the young people who came in to see them about the only way to live a fulfilling and completely satisfying life. The team members provided them with a non-alcoholic drink of some kind and then talked through their life situations with them.

People who had experience of life on the streets and who may possibly have been addicts were in their element in that environment. Kerri wasn't.

As she spoke to some of the people she met on the streets or who came 'on board' she found that many of them were not particularly happy about their entire set-up. What frustrated Kerri was that they didn't seem to want to find out about Jesus even when they were shown the evidence of what He had done for so many already on the bus.

On one occasion she asked a young woman, "Have you ever wanted to get a job?"

Her logic to Kerri was, "Why should I want to get a job? I don't need to work. I get all the money I need to keep me in fags and booze."

This was probably true in her current situation but Kerri wanted to inspire her to think beyond the 'here and now,' to think about what Jesus meant when He said, 'I am the way, the truth and the life,' and His offer of everlasting life in heaven. The woman voiced no objections when Kerri suggested praying for her. That was it, though. That was all. That was as far as she wanted it to go.

There were a small minority, though, who showed a genuine interest in the message of hope and light and peace that the team had come to tell them about. These were the few people who listened intently to the message and, occasionally even in tears, opened their hearts to Jesus.

Kerri finished her six months in the School of Ministry at the end of June but that wasn't the end of her involvement with Teen Challenge. When there she had heard of a mission group going out to India in July and had signed up to be part of the team.

Working in Ammanford had been an easing into outdoor evangelism.

On the streets of Newport she had developed a passion for sharing the good news of Jesus with others.

The Glasgow experience had been a dynamic combination of both demand and reward.

Now what was India going to be like?

# 5

# What If I Die Here?

PEOPLE, PEOPLE, PEOPLE everywhere.

Kerri's first impressions of India were of heat and of people. The humid, clammy heat was stifling and the moving masses of people were almost frightening. It was monsoon season too, and there seemed to be hundreds of bugs of all kinds around plus other unwelcome added-extras like spiders and scorpions.

Julie Murray and her team of eight young women weren't tourists and they were prepared to live under any conditions to achieve their aim. This was to stay in the Women's Centre at the Village of Hope at Ashagram, learn about the work carried out there and afford what assistance they could. They were given a conducted tour of the centre on the day they arrived and met some of the 40 women and girls, who were former drug addicts or prostitutes, who lived there. Life skills classes were in progress at the time and the women seemed to be happily engaged in sewing or making simple leather goods or jewellery.

It was a unique place to be and Kerri reckoned that this was going to be a challenging but very rewarding trip.

The centre at Ashagram is run by Bombay Teen Challenge and on their second day there the group were driven the 60 miles into Mumbai, previously known as

Bombay, a huge city with its 13 million inhabitants. As they looked out from the minibus while passing through the streets and alleys of the city's Kamatipura district they could barely believe the conditions that existed there. The streets were filthy and heaving with people. Tiny children played around large piles of horrible stinking rubbish. Faces peered, sometimes three or four at a time, out of the windows of ramshackle buildings. Teenage girls wearing brightly coloured jangle-bangles that contrasted sharply with their sad dark eyes, paraded up and down the streets or stood on street corners.

Their driver and guide gave them some horrifying statistics as they drove up one dirty street and down another, "There are reckoned to be somewhere in the region of 20,000 prostitutes in these eleven streets alone," he said, "and at least 30% of them will be children." A shiver shot up Kerri's spine and her skin turned to gooseflesh. She felt overcome by a mixture of anger and sad hopelessness.

"Thank you, God that those walls are there," she thought as they passed yet more rows of shabby dwellings, with people coming and going from them ceaselessly. She was scared to know what was possibly going on behind them.

At one stage on their 'tour' they saw a number of young girls being ushered into a taxi and driven away for their 'services.' These were the kind of people that Bombay Teen Challenge was trying to help. They encouraged them out of this cycle of abuse and misery in which they had become entrapped, by offering them a place in the centre at Ashagram. Those taking up the offer would be helped adjust into normal life through a programme of training in 'life skills' and they would also be told the good news of Jesus Christ. The group from Wales would be going back on to the streets another day to make contact with some of them.

To be honest Kerri wasn't overly enthusiastic about the prospect. She found the place disturbing. All she wanted to do at that moment was return to the centre as quickly as possible.

She soon settled into the routine at the Women's House. The programme that the team had prepared was so warmly received that they were able to ignore the rain and the mud and the unwelcome presence of all the creeping creatures, especially the scorpions. Before leaving for India Julie had given each member of the group a subject on which she was to speak during the daily Bible teaching sessions.

The theme of the talks was 'Women of the Bible' and Kerri's topic was the woman whom the scribes and Pharisees brought before Jesus in John chapter 8.

Having had time to prepare, Kerri called her talk, 'Throwing the First Stone' and started by passing sheets of paper to every girl present, both team members and girls from the House. Kerri then asked them to write on as many sheets as they wanted the name of any sins they could think of, and crumple them up into balls. Those, she told them, were each girl's 'stones,' which they were to start throwing at each other when she gave the shout.

This was fun and everyone enjoyed trying to hit each other with their paper 'stones.' Kerri soon called all the excitement to a halt and outlined how pointless this all was as each girl was being bombarded by 'stones' from the others. She highlighted the fact that we are all sinful beings by the way we have turned our backs on God and chosen to ignore Him. This is evident by the outward sins we commit, and no one is in a position to judge anyone else.

Kerri wrapped up the study by passing around the bin and asking all the girls to throw their 'stones' into it. This, she said, was an illustration of how that, although we have all sinned, Jesus, represented by the bin, came to take away our sin if we choose to trust Him to deal with it. She explained that He welcomed everybody who came to Him, no matter what their condition, or how despised they might be by a self-righteous society.

It was such a pleasure to teach these women and girls. They sat listening so intently to every word.

The same thing happened in the English classes, which Kerri helped teach almost every day. The girls were so keen to learn. Their plea at the end of each lesson was, "Please can we do more? Can you give us homework for tomorrow?"

If the centre experience was a joy and delight the street work experience was more of a trial. Kerri went along in a group with some of the others in the team who had once been drug addicts and could identify with the abuse and addictions that the girls they contacted were living with. It was strange, but Kerri, who had a very different life experience, one of achievement and success, felt unsure and uncomfortable here. She remained in the background to allow the more experienced and confident women to 'front' their initiative. Kerri assumed the role of back up, and was happy to pray with some of the girls when this was required.

It was the beginning of their second week in India and Kerri was relishing every minute of her English teaching and doing what she could on the outreach teams, when she felt unwell one morning. She became increasingly out of sorts as the day went on and when it came time for her evening class she found it difficult to concentrate on the lesson. Her legs had become weak and shaky and she felt sick. Kerri completed her teaching and left early to go back to her room. When others returned to the room she said, "I don't feel well. I feel really dizzy!"

Cher either didn't hear, or chose to ignore Kerri's declaration of dizziness, for her eyes had become firmly fixed on her friend's forehead. "Oh my goodness Kerri, what's that lump on your face?!" she exclaimed. "Are you O.K.? Are you taking a reaction to something?"

What was the girl talking about? Kerri found a hand mirror in the room and on looking in it discovered that there was indeed a large red lump on her forehead. By then her breathing was affected and her throat had started to swell up. She began to feel even worse.

Kerri lay down on her bed and Nadine, another of the girls who was sharing the room with her, came in. "You look dreadful, Kerri," she remarked.

"I'm finding it hard to breathe," came the reply. Kerri had never been one for making a big fuss about anything but this inability to breathe was becoming distressing. She went on, "Maybe you had better tell somebody, Nadine."

It was the first time that Julie, the team leader, had left the group as she had gone into a nearby town to shop for supplies, but Nadine, and another of her roommates, Jill, were able to take action.

They found Joyce, the Indian lady in charge of the House of Hope and she brought up their nurse who had only been in the job for a month. Both of these women considered calling the doctor they had all visited a few days before but then remembered that the phones hadn't been working for the last two days!

So it was down to the relatively inexperienced nurse. She came and looked more closely at Kerri before asking a few questions in her very broken English and then leaving with the promise that she would return shortly.

As Kerri lay on the bed gazing up at the ceiling, she was looking but not seeing very clearly. Everything was beginning to go out of focus. Breathing was becoming even more difficult and she began to think of the outcome of this rapidly deteriorating situation, if somebody didn't come, or something didn't happen, soon. Tears of despair welled up in her eyes and overflowed down the sides of her cheeks on to her pillow.

"What if I die here?" she panicked. "I can't breathe, and when you can't breathe you die!"

Feeling that she was fast approaching the point where she was about to seize up completely and die, she reasoned, 'So what if I really do die?'

Her mind went racing. ' I'm only 23 years old, but I could die here and now in India! Is life this fragile? Is this it? Will it end for me here away from my family and close friends? What will they think? What will they do?'

She was conscious that Jill, who had stayed with her, was praying for her and then her mind went down another track not bounded by fear and panic.

Kerri thought about God and remembered His promises. Jesus died that I might have life...everlasting life in heaven. What could be better than that? Her fear had subsided and the overwhelming assurance of somewhere far greater than here gripped her heart and made her smile. An immense sense of peace enveloped her.

'Actually,' she pondered slowly, 'whatever happens to me, I know that God is with me. It is all in His hands and will be what He wants for me. Whether I go to heaven in five minutes or fifty years time, it's OK because God has got me.'

After that Kerri closed her eyes and said a silent prayer, "God, you've got me," she began. "Thank You. I am Yours. Whatever happens to me now I know You've got me. I am Yours."

Sporting prowess didn't matter now. Kerri felt so dizzy and sick that she couldn't have thought about hitting a squash ball.

Beauty contests were a distant memory. Kerri's face now had a horrendous lump on it and her lips were dry and cracked.

University degrees were of no consequence here. Kerri was depending on a couple of reconstituted drug addicts to do what they could for her.

This was about determining priorities in life. And in the face of death Kerri had identified her single top priority. God. Living for Him, or dying for Him, it was all about Him.

After what seemed like an age to Kerri and Jill the nurse returned to Kerri's side. She could see at once that the young woman on the bed was very ill, and decided to give her an injection straight away.

While the nurse was there the girls in the room tried the phone again and to their amazement it worked. It had been out of order for two days but was now back in operation. They were able to make contact with the clinic and when the doctor taking the message sensed the urgency in the voice of the caller, he and his wife came to where Kerri was as soon as possible.

The doctor's wife put an ice pack on Kerri's head while he made his diagnosis. He concluded that she was suffering an allergic reaction and needed hospital treatment. The nurse and Kerri's roommates helped her out to the doctor's car and he and his wife drove her to the nearest hospital.

Tears ran down Kerri's cheeks as she half-lay half-sat in the car on the way to hospital. They weren't tears for herself though. It was her family she was thinking about now. Kerri felt happy in her relationship with God. He had her in His strong and loving arms. Her Heavenly Father was cradling His child like a tiny helpless baby, but what would her parents do if she died out here in India? They didn't even know she was ill. And they didn't even have the chance to say their last goodbye.

All she could do was pray for them. In the middle of all her physical and emotional distress she prayed and thanked God for her parents, her brothers and sister.

When Kerri arrived at the hospital in the doctor's car, Julie was waiting for her. The other girls had contacted her and she had gone straight to the hospital. This was reassuring. Julie had trained and practised as a nurse before changing profession to work for Teen Challenge and was able to set Kerri's mind at rest.

"Don't worry, Kerri. Everything is going to be OK," she told her more than once. "You are in God's hands. He is looking after you."

Kerri knew that. At the very darkest moment of that traumatic evening she had come to recognise that she had no control over her own condition and that her breath, whether it stopped or stayed, was totally a matter for God,

A hospital doctor gave her another injection and a nurse came to insert a drip in her arm. Despite her weak condition Kerri was alert enough to wonder, after her short experience of working with drug addicts, and all the talk she had heard about the prevalence of Aids, where the needle had been.

There was no problem, however. Everything was clinically clean and within an hour Kerri began to feel better. The staff insisted that she remain overnight in the hospital for observation nonetheless and Julie stayed with her.

Neither girl felt like sleeping and so they talked and prayed together through the silent hours of the night. Kerri shared how she had come to realise that knowing God, was all that really mattered and anything else that had been taking His place in her life would have to go.

When she grew a little stronger Kerri needed the bathroom. As she walked gingerly along the corridor pushing her drip, with Julie leading the way holding a spluttering candle, she cast her mind back over the previous six or seven hours. 'Look at this,' she mused. 'Everything is so peaceful again. The trauma is over. All is back to normal. Isn't God amazing?' This reflection was followed by another personal pledge to God to make Him her Number One.

Kerri's first concern on being discharged from hospital the following morning was to let her parents know the latest news. A phone call to her mum let the family know she had been in hospital with 'an allergic reaction to something,' but that she was OK now. She was careful to play down the potentially serious nature of the incident to avoid undue worry back home. With her parents acquainted with the position, and her body gradually recovering its strength Kerri felt a lot better when she rejoined the team that afternoon.

The day before the group of girls from Teen Challenge UK was due to leave for home there was a baptismal service in the Village of Hope. Almost 50 young women were due to make a public confession of their faith in Christ in an open-air service. That was a memorable day for it was spent in prayer and praise. When the girls were baptised in a tank that was home to a colony of frogs and an assortment of other water creatures the atmosphere of the joy and peace and presence of God was almost tangible.

It was an inspirational experience both for the girls who were being baptised and the team from Wales who had come to know and love so many of them. Kerri, who was by then much stronger, revelled in the God-centred tone of it all. Looking back, she had also loved the English teaching and had learnt so much about herself and about relating to others for Jesus, on the streets and alleys of Kamatipura.

The most life-affecting experience of all, though, was when she threw herself into the hands of her God, to do with her as He pleased.

'I could die here,' she had thought, firmly believing it but yet at peace with it.

It had been a testing time, which God had brought her through. He had other plans for her and Kerri left India with a singular resolve for Him.

She wanted to make God uppermost in her life from then on, in everything and forever.

# 6

# Go For It!

SOON AFTER RETURNING from India, Kerri started as an engineer for a large international company in Bristol and then soon transferred to their main London office. It was while working there one morning in spring 2006 that a notice on the internal e-mail system caught her attention.

The BBC was recruiting a team of 15 volunteers from a variety of professions and trades within the construction industry. They planned to film the building of an eco-lodge and the initial stages of setting up an animal conservancy in Kenya. A brief job description was included and anyone interested was invited to send for an application form.

It sounded like a great opportunity to use her skills to help others and it had an appealing air of adventure about it. Kerri forwarded the e-mail to each of her two brothers to gauge their reaction. 'I like the idea of this. What do you think?' she asked.

Martin replied immediately. His counsel could not have been clearer. 'Go for it!' he simply wrote back.

Kerri didn't need any further encouragement and she requested an application form, completed it, returned it and committed the matter to God.

It wasn't long after that when she was contacted out of the blue for a telephone interview. It was at 4.30 in the afternoon and Kerri had been out of the office all day on a course, which had finished early. During the half-hour call she felt quite relaxed and was able to give more detail about the information already stated on the application form. Her attitude and answers must have been satisfactory for she was invited to attend an interview, in front of television cameras, in Bristol in mid-July.

This took place during her summer holiday from work. Kerri had already gone across to Northern Ireland to prepare for a Christians in Sport Camp at which she was helping as a leader. She had to return to Bristol on a Friday, the day camp was due to start, for the interview. Kerri had no problems finding her way around the city as she had already worked there for a time.

It was slightly more daunting to be interviewed in front of the big cameras than over the telephone but Kerri answered all she was asked and felt she had done the best she could. Having learnt that there were hundreds of applicants for the 15 places on offer she was pleased to have reached the final interview stage. She was happy to leave the outcome to God - and the panel from the BBC. They knew the kind of person they needed for the project and God knew what was best for her. It was one of those times when she totally trusted God, even though she so much wanted to be picked.

After the interview Kerri spent the afternoon with some friends she had met while working in Bristol, returned to Belfast, helped at the camp and then went back to work in London the following week. With all that had happened in between, Kerri had almost forgotten about her interest in the Kenyan adventure until she received a telephone call from the BBC one day.

"We would like to offer you a place on our Mission Africa team," she was told.

It was exciting news, but Kerri knew that she would still have to ask her employers for leave to go. She explained this to the Mission Africa coordinator and was told that they would like her to confirm her place within two days. If she wasn't able to join the group then someone else would have to take her place. Time was of the essence because they wanted to make final arrangements for the trip.

Kerri was thrilled. It seemed like a wonderful opportunity. She had been selected as one of 15 to travel to Africa where she could use her engineering skills and experience to help develop a worthwhile venture from scratch. With the first hurdle of selection complete, the second hurdle of obtaining leave from work presented itself.

When she told her manager about the offer she had received, and the response deadline, he said that he needed time to think it over. His decision, two days later was, "I'm sorry, Kerri, but we can't afford to let you go."

This was understandable from a business point of view but a shock and a setback to Kerri. She went home that evening not convinced that this ought to be the final outcome. Her mind was beset with questions. Was this not one thing she had always dreamed of doing? Had God not planned this opportunity for her? Did He not want her to do it after all?

It was a frustrating situation. What should she do?

She phoned her mum that evening, asking for her advice, and then she called Steph, a Christian friend and fellow engineer from university, whose counsel she trusted. Her problem was that she had been told she couldn't go, but the more she thought about it the more she wanted to go!

Prayer times came before, between and after telephone calls. Kerri's prayer was that God would guide her in this situation, as she wanted to be an honourable employee, but also true to her natural instincts and His will.

Late in the evening, having wrestled long and hard with the problem she eventually made up her mind, obtained the telephone number of her manager, and called him. She reminded him of her Mission Africa opportunity and then went on to state her position. It was simply that she had decided to go on the trip to Kenya whether it meant giving up her job or not.

The manager said that he would have to discuss it with a more senior boss in the office the next morning. He told Kerri, whose two-day deadline had already passed, to come and see him the following afternoon as she had meetings out of the office in the morning.

It was a bold step to take and Kerri didn't sleep much that night. Have I done the right thing, or have I made a big mistake here? The pros and cons of the choice she had made tormented her as she lay awake.

Her first appointment the next morning was in Greenwich and having taken the tube out there she found that she had half an hour to spend before going into the meeting. It was a sunny, warm, July morning and Kerri sat down on a park bench to wait. She was sitting outside the David Beckham Sports Academy and groups of young people, football boots in hand, were being dropped off by their parents to start their day's training.

Kerri watched them for a few moments before taking a Bible from her bag and turning to the book of Psalms. In addition to her daily Bible reading, Kerri often turned to the Psalms in times of need. They had proved a source of comfort and inspiration to her before and she prayed they would do so again.

She had read a few different places before turning over to Psalm 16  As she began reading through it, several verses really made her sit up.

'You are my Lord; apart from you I have no good thing,' she read.

Farther down she came upon the wonderful assurance, 'I have set the Lord always before me. Because he is at my right hand, I shall not be shaken.'

'You have made known to me the path of life...'

As Kerri thought over the words of the Psalm she realised that whatever happened about the Mission Africa situation, God's gift of Jesus and life is far greater and His plan for her life is far better that anything she could ever dream up. So she closed her eyes and prayed, "Thank You, Lord. I give You my life again and I trust that You know best what to do with it. Just help me to be pleased with whatever You choose to do, knowing that it is Your best for me and thus my best also."

Kerri went into the business meeting in Greenwich with a tremendous peace in her heart. She was trusting God. He was in control.

On returning to the head office that afternoon she went to see the manager she had talked to the night before on the phone.

"Did you get a chance to speak to the others?" she enquired.

"Yes, I did, Kerri," he replied. "You know that this is a very important job you are working on at the moment."

There was a short pause and Kerri's heart began to sink. What was coming next? "But have a good time. We hope it goes well for you," he went on.

Kerri was taken by surprise at this different approach and asked, hesitantly, "Does that mean I will still have a job when I come back?"

"Yes. We will see you when your six weeks is up," came the reply.

When she rang the BBC to claim her place on the trip she found someone there rather concerned. "You are the last one to phone in, Kerri," they said, "but we are glad you are able to come. You will be receiving your gear from us within the next week or two."

Those were exciting days of anticipation and preparation. Her work colleagues were very supportive as she kept them informed of each new phase in the build up. That could include anything from going for inoculations to checking through and trying on the range of clothing supplied. Kerri also included a cap and tee shirt from the company that had granted her leave to go on the trip. She thought that perhaps she might be able to wear them 'on camera' sometime.

While busy making all the practical arrangements, Kerri realised that this trip could be an influential time in her relationship with God. It was six weeks away from everyone she knew and possibly without any Christian support at all. The prospect scared her at times, for this would be another chapter 'out of the norm' of life, where it would become evident how strong her relationship with God really was.

She had wanted to put Him first ever since her illness in India, but had she really?

Would she still think about God, love Him and try to glorify Him in all she did when she was away?

The party, led by Ken Hyams and Nick Knowles, assembled at Heathrow Airport en route for Kenya. The group of young adults, all with experience in some aspect of the construction industry had been recruited from various locations across the UK to contribute his or her particular skill to their 'Mission Africa' challenge. There was a subdued excitement, an unspoken expectation, as they added their personal baggage to the enormous pile of camera equipment ready to be checked on board the flight.

On arrival in Africa the 15 volunteers caught another internal flight over Mount Kenya and were subsequently driven miles into the Kenyan bush. By the time they arrived at their destination it was too late to start putting up the tents. The only option was for everyone to roll out their sleeping bags and camp beds and sleep under the stars. This was a testing time since the group were still only at that awkward, early, sizing-one-another-up stage in the adventure, with tiredness and unfamiliar surroundings all mounting up.

After lugging numerous bags across a dry riverbed and eating food out of their mess tins the party settled down for some much-needed sleep. With the strange noises of the night and reports of a herd of elephants feeding close by, however, very few of them felt relaxed enough to close an eye until dawn broke across the plains.

Kerri began her night below the open sky by praying in her sleeping bag. She asked God for the courage and discernment to know best how to represent Him in this situation. She had asked her Christian friends, before leaving England, to pray for her when in Kenya and she felt sure that they were doing so. It was great to feel the strength of the unity of the Christian faith though thousands of miles apart.

She had always found it easy to get to sleep, and in contrast to most of the rest of the group Kerri soon drifted off and had a good six-hour kip.

The first few days were difficult. They were spent establishing camp, identifying what specialities each team member could contribute, delegating responsibilities and getting to know one another. Kerri thought it would be great when they started to make some visible progress on the actual project, but that was still some way ahead.

They had arrived at their campsite on a Wednesday evening and on Sunday morning Kerri was thinking that if she was back in London she would be going to church today. During the course of the day she talked to some of the Kenyan workers and asked them about their usual Sunday routines. She was pleased to discover that a few of them were Christians so they agreed to read the Bible and pray that evening before dinner.

This was an encouraging development, and so before dinner one of the Kenyan workers read the Bible, another talked about the verses that had been read, and Kerri prayed.

Dinner that evening was a Kenyan speciality, freshly cooked goat, and Kerri was touched afterwards when a fellow apprentice came over to her as they dispersed. "Thanks very much. That was very good," he said most sincerely. Kerri's short and simple prayer had helped establish her Christian identity in the camp and created openings for her to talk to the others about God in the weeks that were to follow.

On the construction side of things one of the immediate priorities for the group was to pipe a sustainable supply of fresh water to the building site. This was essential for the building work they were planning to do and would be vital in the running of the animal conservancy.

Kerri, and Scott, a water engineer, were assigned the challenge of setting up a system that would bring water on to the site from some distance away. Until then another apprentice had been given the punishing task of maintaining a useable water reserve by carrying it to a container on the site in buckets from a nearby well in the searing African heat.

They had problems and setbacks but eventually they got the water flowing and everybody was delighted. This was going to facilitate the building project and when the water began to flow freely through the pipe everyone present was sprayed with water in celebration!

The pipe lying on top of the ground was impractical and dangerous, so the next assignment was to dig a narrow shallow trench in which to bury it. The camera crews were in place to record this stage in the proceedings with all the team ready to go. Nick gave the signal to start and Kerri drove the first strike with her pick straight into the water pipe they had just laid! A fountain of precious water gushed about a metre into the air!

Everybody laughed, but their amusement only added to Kerri's embarrassment. Imagine the stupidity of it! Spending days trying to set up a viable water supply and then sabotaging it as soon as they had it working! The mistake was soon forgiven, the pipe mended and the supply restored, but the incident made good television.

Away from the occasional high point of excitement, the mundane hard labour in fifty-degree heat, from eight in the morning until six in the evening every day, gradually began to wear people down. It was a constant battle for Kerri to try and set aside pride, jealousy and at times even bitterness towards the others, and the long draining days often prevented her from spending quality time in Bible reading and prayer.

Halfway through the second week, when she was running low on energy and finding it difficult to keep the joy of knowing God her top priority, Kerri had to stop and really assess the situation. She knew we were called at times to simply be obedient in reading our Bibles even when we don't feel like it, and when she did that she was refreshed. Going back to the basics of knowing who God was and what He had done for her lifted her spirits. It should be a joy to represent Him here in Africa just as anywhere else. What could be more important?

One of Kerri's most frightening experiences during the filming of Mission Africa was when she went out as part of a tracking team one afternoon. The Kenyan rangers and Ken Hyams were instructing the team in the tracking of rhino. Their first stop had been to feed an orphan baby rhino with a bottle and that was fun for all.

The group of five then drove farther out into the bush where the rangers located a mother rhino and her baby. The driver manoeuvred to within a mile or so of the pair and three people were offered the chance to go nearer on foot, under the watchful eye of Ken Hyams and the armed rangers. Jamie, Andrew and Kerri were the first to volunteer to go forward, and leaving the security of their jeep they approached the rhino and her baby for a closer look.

They were looking at the rhinos when they became conscious of a noise behind them. It was a herd of about fifty buffalo and one of these huge, fierce looking creatures had his head down and was stamping and pawing the ground as though preparing to charge.

Kerri, Jamie and Andrew froze in position. What should they do?

The team back in the jeep saw the danger and knew exactly what to do. "We are moving the safety car between you and the buffalo," came the message over the two-way radio. "Get back to the jeep! We are coming to meet you."

The three young volunteers were glad to see the vehicle making its way towards them and when their legs regained enough strength to propel them forward they ran to it as quickly as possible. Once they were safely in the jeep it wheeled around and set off in the opposite direction followed by the safety car, leaving the herd of buffalo and the pair of rhino undisturbed on the plain.

It had been an exciting encounter!

As the project started to take shape Kerri began to enjoy the interaction with the others and the satisfaction of being able to contribute, in a small way to the local community, who would benefit from the conservancy. Her Christian identity led to her having good chats with some of the others about God and other topics relevant to her faith.

The project was completed on time despite a number of last minute hiccups. With the eco-lodge built and a number of wild animals captured in other parts of the country and released on the reserve it was time to hand it all over to the local tribes who were to run it. Members of the team went around the neighbouring villages inviting the residents to an opening ceremony, and they came, colourfully dressed, dancing and singing, along to the site.

Each member of the team was invited to contribute to the programme if he or she wished and there were no objections raised when Kerri asked permission to say a prayer at the opening ceremony. She was well aware that everyone's closing remarks would be recorded on camera for posterity even though it would be impossible to include them all in the course of a half-hour broadcast, and so she chose her words carefully. It was important that what she said should be powerful, accurate and most of all honouring to God.

When it came her turn to speak during the ceremony Kerri said her prayer which she based around the opening words of Psalm 24, 'The earth is the Lord's and everything in it, the world and all who live in it.' She asked for the blessing of God upon the future running of the project and upon the local community and was only halfway through when there was a loud 'Amen.' One of the Kenyan men was obviously in full agreement with the thoughts expressed in her dedicatory prayer and couldn't even wait to the end of it to show his approval!

After the ceremony two people made a point of speaking to Kerri. One of these was another apprentice who commented, "That was really good Kerri. Where did you get that prayer from?"

Kerri replied that prayer is just like talking to God so she had put it together herself.

"That's amazing!" was the apprentice's astonished response.

The other person to come forward to see Kerri was a lady who was among a group of special visitors. "Thank you," she began, "I have never met you before but I knew from the very moment you started to speak that you were a Christian."

Kerri was thrilled to meet her and they introduced themselves to one another. The woman was from Kenya but had spent a lot of time in London and other parts of England. On her last visit to the UK she had actually wanted to go to a big church in London that she had heard about.

Kerri's mouth fell open. "That's where I go now!" she exclaimed.

The two women had so much in common and they were delighted to have met. When the others began celebrating with the food and drink that had been laid on for the ceremony they withdrew to the sidelines and continued their conversation.

Few people paid much attention to the two women sitting together, talking away as though they had been friends for a lifetime, in the starlit African night. One was on a chair provided for the visitors and the other, Kerri, was perched on an upturned crate.

God was watching over them, though. These were His children. He had brought them together in a most unlikely location, aware that each would be an encouragement to the other.

When Kerri arrived back in the UK late the following day she began to reflect on her time away. She had 'gone for it,' as Martin had suggested. She had gone to help establish a game conservancy in Kenya but in doing so had received much more in return. There were times when she had not honoured God but as she continues to grow and mature she aims to make these times fewer.

Going for it, for God. That has been Kerri's sole aim since the day of her baptism, through the trials of India, the challenges of Kenya and the ups and downs of her working and sporting career.

Kerri is still young and continues to pray that God will help her to serve Him for the rest of her life. She has completed another year of engineering and is currently taking leave from work to pursue her dream on the professional squash circuit.

She wants to give herself to God, and the path He has for her, however hard or easy it turns out to be, however near or far it calls her. She recognises that the greatest gift of all is her salvation through Jesus Christ; the gift of true life, so the least she can do is to offer her life, here and now, to Him.

That, she believes, is the only way worth living life.

# Going for it ...
## in the net

# Stuart's
## Story

# 1

# It's OK To Cry You Know, Son!

"I HAVE NO CHANCE here!" thought young Stuart Elliott.

He was sitting in a dressing room at Strandtown Primary School and there seemed to be hundreds of other boys around him. They all looked so much bigger than he did, too, and many of them seemed to know each other.

Stuart didn't know any of them. He was the only boy picked from his school, Mersey Street in east Belfast, to attend the first set of trials to select a Primary School Football Team to represent the city in competitions in both Northern Ireland and England.

He was shivering. He was scared. And he was desperately embarrassed.

He couldn't tie his own bootlaces.

That was when Terry Moore, who was the coach of the Belfast team, spotted his predicament and with a reassuring smile bent down and tied them for him. Even if he didn't play well enough to be selected, that action in itself would have been enough to make ten-year-old Stuart's day. Terry played for Glentoran Football Club, the team he supported, and was one of his boyhood heroes. Stuart and his pal Paul Leeman never missed a match at the Oval, and to have Terry Moore tie his bootlaces was a dream come true!

All his inhibitions melted away when he made it out on to the pitch, however. Stuart loved to play football. He had been doing it with his friends up and down Banbury Street where he lived since shortly after he was able to walk. That was how they spent balmy summer evenings and chilly winter afternoons.

This now was his 'big chance' and he made the most of it. He played the best he could, but since he was one of the smallest boys on the field the thought struck him again as he trooped off with the rest, 'I have no chance here!'

After the match Terry Moore was surrounded by a horde of sweaty boys all anxious to know if they had 'been picked.' The coach consulted a notebook and a few soggy scraps of paper before announcing the names of the thirty players he wanted to see again for further training, and from whom the final squad of fifteen would be selected. One of those names was Stuart Elliott.

Stuart was thrilled. Overjoyed. Over the moon.  As he walked home down the Newtownards Road the evening was becoming colder but he didn't feel it. Darkness was closing in, but he didn't care. He had made it into the final thirty of all the boys playing football in all the Primary Schools in the whole of Belfast. Now he knew how a professional player must feel when he received his first call-up to represent his country in the World Cup!

The next two training sessions were scrappy competitive affairs with thirty boys knowing that they were playing for fifteen places. The only preparation Stuart could make for those matches was to learn to tie his own laces, so he did that. When it came to the matches he played hard and obviously impressed the watching selectors clustered in a small intent group on the touchline. After the second session he was told that he had made it to the final fifteen. Ten-year-old Stuart Elliott was on the Belfast team!

He became the envy of all his team-mates at Mersey Street Primary School and his 'Glens'-supporting pals when he came back to tell of the matches he had played for Belfast against other Primary School teams in Northern Ireland. Then the treat of the year for him was to make his first trip 'across the water' to play for Belfast Primary Schools against Liverpool Primary Schools.

There was another great thrill awaiting him later in the year too. Just when Stuart was sad to think that the football season would soon be over for the summer a strange man appeared in Banbury Street, and came knocking on the Elliot's back door. He was wearing a long coat with a small Glasgow Rangers badge on it, and a hat. This seemed rather odd given that it was the month of May, but there was a reason for this curious dress code. It was to disguise his identity from those who didn't know who he was and to confirm it to those who did.

It was Joe Kincaid, who was the coach of the St. Andrews Boys Club team on the Shankill Road in Belfast and who also acted as Northern Ireland 'scout' for Glasgow Rangers. When someone had gone to see who was standing at the open back door Joe asked if this was 'where young Stuart Elliot lived.' He was assured that it was, and when he asked to speak to his parents was invited in.

There seemed to be children of all ages either standing around in or scurrying out through that small living room when Joe entered it. Stuart was the seventh of a family of ten so there was always somebody around to greet a visitor!

When Stuart was located and told that there was 'a man looking for him' he wondered what this could all be about. As soon as he saw the man in the overcoat, however, he realised that he had seen him before. He had been watching most of the matches in which he had played for the Belfast Primary Schools team.

Joe Kincaid wasted no time in stating the reason for his visit after Stuart had joined his mother and as many of his two brothers and seven sisters as had turned up to see what was going on. Nodding down at Stuart, and then addressing his mum, he said, "I have been watching this boy playing football for a while now. He is small but he has great potential. I was wondering if you would allow him to play for me in St. Andrews Boys Club on the Shankill Road? I am always on the lookout for good players like I think Stuart is going to turn out to be."

Julie Elliot knew how much her Stuart loved his football and had no objections to him playing for St. Andrews or any other football team for that matter as long as it made him happy, and so she gave her consent. Stuart was to start training with St. Andrews in the summer.

Before that though, he was quite unexpectedly awarded his first personal trophy as a footballer. His father, who worked really hard and long in his plumbing business to support his large family, had afforded himself the evening off to take his son Stuart up to the end-of-season awards and celebration evening of the Belfast Primary Schools Football team in Le Mon Hotel. Young Stuart felt so proud that night. He was chuffed to be wearing his green jumper with the Belfast badge on it but he was even mote delighted to have his dad with him. Tommy Elliot had promised to take his talented son to as many matches as possible and Stuart loved him for that.

At the end of the evening Terry Moore stood up with a few cups and trophies on a table in front of him and another, dry this time, sheet of paper in his hand. It was time to present the awards.

Stuart was surprised into shock when, with only one cup left on the table, Terry announced, "And finally we come to the Belfast Primary Schools Football Team Player of the Year award. This goes to the boy with the golden left foot, Stuart Elliot."

There was loud applause from all around and the short legs that had run miles around muddy pitches in representative matches were shaking with excitement as Stuart went up to collect his cup. Things had changed dramatically from that first day when he couldn't tie his own bootlaces and had thought in a boyish panic, 'I have no chance here!'

Things progressed on the same upward spiral as soon as Stuart left Mersey Street Primary School and commenced his secondary school education at Ashfield Boys High School in east Belfast. All he wanted to do, day or night, weekday or weekend, was play football.

He was often playing at least two matches a week. There was a match for a school team, coached by Mr. Ricky McCann, a teacher whom he really liked since he showed a particular interest in him for he recognised his ability, on an afternoon after school. This was followed by a game for St. Andrews under the watchful and critical eye of Joe Kincaid and in the proud and encouraging presence of his dad, on a Saturday morning.

This constant playing exposed Stuart's prowess with his 'golden left foot' to a wide and discerning footballing public and led to him being invited to attend Eddie Coulter's Manchester United School of Excellence. This was yet another dream come true. Now he was associated, however distantly, with one of the world's most respected football clubs. Could he ever end up wearing one of those famous red shirts? It was almost too much to imagine but he dared to imagine it anyway. When it came to the more down-to-earth reality of attending the training sessions, however, it was again his dad that took him across the city to the astro turf pitches at the Olympia Leisure Centre on Boucher Road. He was going to make sure that his son Stuart was given every possible chance to make the best of what Joe Kincaid had described as his 'potential.'

Everything seemed to be on the up-and-up for Stuart until something happened one Saturday that turned the tide against him in a single devastating blow.

Glentoran had no home match that day and so Stuart and his friend Paul had gone to see another east Belfast team, Dundela, play. They were walking home down Mersey Street talking football as usual when Paul's aunt appeared at the doorway of her home. She seemed a bit flustered and said hastily, "Come on in here, Paul. Stuart has to go home."

Paul look puzzled but there was a peculiar sense of concern and urgency in her tone of voice that compelled him to do as she had commanded. With a brief but bewildered shrug of the shoulders and a short, "See you, Stuart," he followed his aunt into the house.

Stuart quickened his step wondering why he 'had to go home.' What had happened? Why did Paul's aunt not seem to want his best mate to come with him?

All the questions that were racing through his mind were answered when he met his uncle Billy just as he turned into Banbury Street. He had an awestruck faraway look about him, which Stuart was soon to discover stemmed from a mixture of grief and disbelief.

"We have been waiting for you to come home, son," he began, and then without waiting for Stuart to make any response he went on to explain. "I hardly know how to tell you but your daddy died of a massive heart attack earlier on there today, in my arms."

Stuart didn't know what to do, or say, or think. He had just turned thirteen years of age and had never experienced death at close quarters before. That single sentence from uncle Billy had the effect of turning his life into a sickening shattering blur.

It was difficult to find anybody to speak to in the house when he arrived at it with uncle Billy. The place was packed with women with red eyes and paper hankies and men with long solemn white faces. He pushed his way in and eventually found his mum who took him in her arms and sobbed softly.

An endless stream of people passed through the house that weekend, anxious to convey words of condolence to Julie Elliott, many of them assuring her that she and the family would be 'in their thoughts and prayers.' It also seemed to be part of the patter to describe her husband Tommy as a 'good man who loved his family and worked hard to provide for them.'

That was true. As Stuart sat in a corner in a daze with his brothers and sisters watching the mourners come and go he thought back three or four days to the previous Thursday night. That was when he had overheard his dad say to his mum with a degree of satisfaction, "I have landed a good wee bit of business today, Julie. It will be enough to keep us going for a good while."

He had been pleased for him, and for all of them, too. His dad had worked every hour he could on every 'job' he could get, to help support his family. Now that 'good wee bit of business' he had 'landed' would never be done.

A creeping fear began to chill Stuart's mind. Their breadwinner had gone. What was going to happen to them now? How would mother manage? And what would happen to them if the same thing happened to her?

It was a very large funeral, boosted by the appearance of many of Stuart's teammates from the cross-community St. Andrews Boys Club. They all turned up in their track-suits and Stuart was glad to see them but totally at a loss to know what to say to them when they told him that they were 'sorry to hear about your daddy." He bit his lip, said very little, and tried not to cry. After all he was thirteen and a would-be big-man footballer, and big-men footballers didn't cry.

When the funeral was over Joe Kincaid turned up at the Elliot's back door again, dressed in that same long overcoat. Stepping into the kitchen to see the young player that he was hopefully grooming for greatness, he told him that he had come to say how sorry he was to hear about the death of the loyal dad he had met at the matches. Stuart looked up at him, grim-faced and tight-lipped and nodded his appreciation.

Joe Kincaid, sensing what was going on in the teenager's head reached over, placed a hand on his shoulder and said, "It's OK to cry you know, son."

That was a relief to know and immediately the pent-up emotions of the past days all seemed to end up in Stuart's eyes, sending huge tears rolling down his cheeks. Knowing that this was what the young lad really needed Joe let him weep. When he regained a measure of composure the coach assured him, "Your place is waiting for you Stuart. Come back when you are ready,"

It was hard to go back, however, for Stuart didn't want to leave his mother. He felt, as did the rest of the family, that he ought to be with her as much as he could, supporting her in every possible way.

After about a three-month lay-off Stuart was back playing again, though, both for St. Andrews and Ashfield Boys High School. His mum had encouraged him to return to his football, as she knew that it was all young Stuart wanted to do. He in turn began to dream once again, as his teams began to win trophy after trophy, that perhaps he could make a career in football. He pictured himself becoming provider, for he could maybe end up helping to support his mum 'and the others' by 'making loads of money.' It was all a teenage pipedream but it kept him going.

St. Andrews Boys Club won the Northern Ireland Championships three years in a row and Ashfield won the Northern Ireland Secondary Schools Competition one year. The St. Andrews side also played against cup-winning Boys' Club teams from all over Europe in Holland in the Amsterdam Cup Competition. When they went on to win this tournament it was assumed that most of that squad would make it 'into the big time.'

Stuart went to the leaving dinner for St. Andrews Boys Club on the Shankill Road with high hopes. This was when Joe Kincaid would be able to tell the team he had selected and trained over their secondary school career if any local senior, or even better, cross channel, clubs had expressed an interest in them.

He came away bitterly disappointed, though, sick in his stomach. Some of the other lads were told that the managers of well-known clubs would 'be in touch with them about contracts. There was no news of anybody having any interest in getting in touch with Stuart about anything.

'It must be something to do with my size' he kept trying to console himself on the way back home across the city. Joe had told him more than once when playing for St. Andrews, "Always remember, Stuart. Those boys aren't any better than you, they are just bigger." And if an impressive physical presence and not just skill on the ball was to be the determining factor in the future of aspiring footballers he had no chance. He wasn't going to make it. He couldn't grow a foot taller and put on a stone weight overnight! It just wasn't going to happen.

Stuart Elliott left school at sixteen with no qualifications of any sort. He hadn't been interested in lessons. All he had gone to school for was to play football. All he had lived for was playing football. He had come to believe that his trusty left foot would open the door to a career in football and now football had shoulder-charged him out. He felt a failure too, as far as his family was concerned. His vision of helping his mum, who was battling to make ends meet, had been blown to bits.

Before long the school-leaver had begun to wallow in a quagmire of self-pity and recrimination. He spent days just lying about the house hindering and worrying the mum whom he had wanted to help, doing very little. Although he hated the dark nights he would be found out prowling around the streets alone and confused.

What am I here for? he asked himself.

What's the point of anything? he wanted to know.

Why am I such a walking disaster? I have let my dead dad, my struggling mum and my useless self down and I haven't a clue what to do about it.

Stuart was waking up every morning to face another empty day thinking that there must be more to life than this. If there wasn't, what was the good of even bothering to go on with it?

You've no chance here, you're no good here, it's OK to cry, had come back to haunt him, big time.

# 2

# Lovely Young Lady

LIFE WAS ONE big long bore.

Stuart Elliott had always dreamt of becoming a professional footballer. He was sixteen years old, had a Schoolboy Player of the Year award, a collection of medals and a 'sweet left foot.' Despite all of that, his career, which appeared to be taking off at breakneck speed, had come crashing to a halt. He was 'too small.'

It was sickening and made him bitter and angry. Where did he go from here? He wasn't interested in taking any kind of a job for he didn't have a qualification to his name.

One evening Stuart called round to see his mate Paul Leeman, just for something different to do, and Paul had just heard something that he was sure might interest his friend. Stuart felt the faintest glow of hope begin to flicker within him when Paul said, "Did you know that Glentoran are starting an under–17 team? There is a practice for it next week. You ought to go round."

Well why not? Stuart thought. I might be 'too small' but I still want to play. There can be no harm in going along and letting them see what I can do with a ball.

He went to the training session of the soon to be formed under-17 team with no real expectations. His self-esteem had already taken a horrible pounding and he didn't want to build up his hopes, only to have them dashed.

Paul Kirk, the Glentoran youth team manager was there and he approached Stuart after that first appearance on the training ground. "Would you like to play for this new team we are starting?" he asked.

Suddenly Stuart had something to live for again. He joined the team and played in every match. Before the end of the season they had established themselves as 'the team to beat' and won the league.

During the summer of 1995 Stuart was walking along the Black Path on his way to a Glentoran training session one evening and passed a large tent on the King George VI Playing Fields. A sign said that a special summer mission conducted by Pastor James McConnell was being held there and gave starting and finishing dates.

His curiosity was aroused by this and when he was invited to a 'Fun Day' on the Saturday of the first week he went along to see what it was all about. Stuart hadn't been long moving around the field until he noticed something striking. It was the joy and enthusiasm which shone from the faces of the people at the different activities that impressed him. This was something he had never come across before, but something he coveted.

These people are 'the real deal' he thought. What was their secret?

When Stuart found Johnny Brown sitting alone in the 'information' caravan he went in and started to talk to him. It wasn't very long into the conversation until Stuart had asked the question that had been puzzling him for the past half-hour or so.

"Why is everybody round here so happy looking?" he enquired.

"What they have is not religion," Johnny began to explain. "It's found in a person. They have peace in their hearts because they have a living relationship with their Saviour, the Lord Jesus."

This was a revelation to Stuart. He had gone to different Sunday Schools around east Belfast as a boy and heard about Jesus, but he hadn't seen this before. A collection of people whose lives seemed to be controlled by Him.

Johnny didn't wait for any response from Stuart before pressing the matter further. "Jesus died on the cross to take the punishment for your sins," he went on, "and if you trust in Him you will be saved from a lost eternity. That's what these people have that you are talking about. It's having Jesus in their hearts that has made the difference."

Stuart had another question for him at that point and interrupted with it. "Hold on, you said that Jesus died. If He is dead how can he make any difference to me or anybody else for that matter?" he wanted to know.

"Yes, He died, but He rose again from the dead, and He is alive for evermore," Johnny continued the story. "That is why He can live in people's lives and make a mighty change in them."

This was a lot for Stuart to take in. Johnny went on to explain the main points of what he called 'the Gospel message.' Stuart listened for a while and then decided it was time he was going. Johnny's last words were to invite him to 'come back and hear Pastor McConnell in the tent some night.'

"Aye, I might," was Stuart's non-committal answer. He wasn't going to promise anything. This stuff about Jesus was all very well but he didn't reckon that he needed to do anything about it just yet. And anyway there were training sessions to be attended and summer-league matches to be played during the week. He would hardly have time to go.

Although trying to convince himself that he didn't need to go into the tent on the playing fields he couldn't escape its influence. As he walked past it on his way home from training he heard Pastor McConnell's voice as he delivered his message to the large audience. Stuart always tried to walk on by but he couldn't. Something that he could neither explain nor control always slowed him down and then brought him to a complete stop.

An inner conviction told him that he ought to slip in at the back and hear more about Jesus and being saved and how to go about with a calm confidence on your face that reflected contentment in your heart.

This was always overcome immediately by another stronger, louder, more insistent voice, which held him back. What would you want to go in there for? it wanted to know. What would your mates think? You want to be a professional footballer one day. Professional footballers aren't religious nuts. Go back to your mates on the street corner.

Despite all the feelings that he should go into the tent some night, he never did. Instead he always gave in to the thought of 'what his mates would say if he turned 'good livin'' as they talked about, and joined them on the street corner.

Stuart couldn't understand what was happening to him. A full-scale tug of war had begun in his heart. He firmly believed that what Johnny Brown had been talking about and Pastor McConnell was preaching about every night was right. He was being pulled towards it by some sort of an irresistible force, and knew he ought to do something about it, but he was scared.

The mission finished and the tent disappeared but the restlessness remained in Stuart's mind. He had no peace in his heart. If the 'Gospel message', as he had picked up bits of it, were true, then it could hold the answers to all the questions he had been asking for the past year and more about the meaning and purpose of life. Yet he hadn't bothered to do anything about it.

Had he missed his chance to be saved? This thought was even more worrying. It was frightening in fact. What was that thing Johnny had been talking about -'a lost eternity?'

When some of the lads that Stuart had met at the Fun Day invited him to go along with them to hear Pastor McConnell preach in Whitewell Metropolitan Tabernacle on Sunday September 3, 1995, he agreed to go. There were two plus points about this as far as Stuart was concerned. The first was that he was going to hear 'the Gospel' in the comfort of a church as opposed to standing dithering outside a tent. The other was that 'Whitewell' was on the other side of the city from where he lived and if whatever he heard there didn't appeal to him in any way then he could just go back to his mates as normal. They weren't even going to know that he had been.

The atmosphere in the church was warm and inviting when Stuart and his friends found seats in the gallery. There was music playing and there seemed to be hundreds of people streaming in to all parts of the building. By the time the service started the two-thousand-seat sanctuary was full.

Stuart was practically overawed by it all. Why would this many people want to come to church?

The worship songs that everyone seemed to be singing so heartily at the beginning were all strange to him. He didn't join in the singing, choosing rather to soak up the mood while looking around at others still trying to find seats.

At the back of his mind there was always the question of 'what is a boy like you doing in a place like this?' It was hard to answer that, other than to acknowledge that he had felt virtually coerced to come by a curious compelling conviction.

When Pastor McConnell started to speak Stuart was moved. He talked about heaven and hell. He told his congregation that where they spent eternity, that was

Johnny's word, depended on each one of them, as individuals. Those who had trusted Christ and were saved would be in heaven and those who rejected Him and 'went their own way' would end up in hell. It was as simple as that. The choice was theirs.

Towards the end of his address he urged those of his audience who weren't Christians to 'come to Christ tonight.' That was the only way they could 'know their sins forgiven and be sure of a home in heaven.'

When Pastor McConnell came to make his appeal at the close of the service Stuart was ready to respond. Bowing his head where he sat he prayed inwardly, 'Lord I want to trust You. I want You to come into My life and change me and help me to live for You."

Leaning forward, with his head still half-bowed Stuart raised his hand high in the air. He didn't care who saw him now. He had made his choice.

Like many teenagers at that time Stuart had allowed his hair to grow long like some of the popular international footballers of the day. This led Pastor McConnell to make an understandable mistake when he caught a glimpse of the flowing locks below the raised hand.

"There is a lovely young lady in the gallery up there," he announced to the hushed congregation. "God bless you."

Stuart's friends were amused at this, but he didn't care. He was sure that something marvellous had happened to him. This had been the right thing to do. This was what he had been looking for all his life. This was what had made the friendly Fun-day organisers look so happy.

Now he had it himself! Wonderful!

That was Stuart's first time in the Metropolitan Tabernacle but it certainly wasn't going to be his last. He couldn't get there often enough after that! He wanted to go to every service he could and he loved to tell others about the new life he had found in Christ.

A total transformation had taken place in his life. When he was at home in east Belfast he was either in the house reading his new Bible or out on the streets giving out tracts, and talking to everybody who would listen, about Jesus. The mates with whom he had once hung around the street corners soon dropped off when he began to witness to them about his newly found faith.

This didn't worry Stuart. His interests and desires had completely changed. Standing in Whitewell on a Sunday night with two thousand others singing 'As the deer pants for the water so my heart runs after You,' and meaning it with all his heart, had now become one of his chief delights.

Stuart's football career was taking off too. When the opportunity arose he told all the players and staff at Glentoran that he was a Christian. Jesus was his Saviour and Lord and He was the controlling influence in his life. This meant that he would be more committed to playing well, to giving it his all, for he was serving a new Master.

Johnny Jamieson, one of Glentoran's famous players, recognised Stuart's talent and helped nurture him along. A big break for him came when he was included in the Glentoran Reserves team to play against Lisburn Distillery Reserves. That was just the start of it, for having played well in the match Stuart retained his place in the reserves for the rest of the season and the team won the reserve league.

It was in the summer of 1996, and at the start of another season, when Stuart achieved one of the dreams of his boyhood days. That was when he made his debut for the Glentoran senior team against Dungannon Swifts at the Oval. He had bowed his head in the dressing room before the match and asked God to help him and then as he walked out on to the turf at the Oval he felt a lump come in his throat. He had been sneaking into matches at this ground since before he had even gone to school, and all throughout his boyhood and teenage years he had cheered on 'the Glens.'

Now here he was, a Glentoran player. To hear the crowd roaring him on was an exhilarating experience and when he scored a header in extra time to win the match he could barely believe it! God had certainly answered his pre-match request. This was 'Roy of the Rovers' stuff!

Suddenly Stuart Elliott had become a household name among Glentoran fans and in the sporting press. The young man, who had once thought that his career in football was finished was now doing radio and television interviews! When his picture appeared in the local papers over the weekend he was knocked for six! This was awesome!

Having cemented his place in the first team Stuart was now faced with another challenge. This time it was one of life and witness. His teammates liked to go out for a drink after training but Stuart had no interest whatsoever in joining them. He had already told them that his life had changed since trusting Jesus and all he wanted to do in the evenings was get home as soon as possible. There he would continue where he had left off studying some Bible passage or character, or listen to a tape or watch a video of a service in Whitewell Metropolitan Tabernacle. Football had become an important part of his life once again but living for God and attending that church were what provided him with his underlying zest for living, his zeal for everything.

It was at 'Whitewell' too that Stuart was to take another positive step into the will of God for his life. His younger sister Kristin was also a member of the church and accompanied him to many of the services there and as they were walking down the stairs together in the slowly-moving crowd after a service one Sunday evening Stuart caught the eye of an attractive girl. As they edged forward he found it hard to stop glancing over in her direction. The strange thing was that every time he looked towards her she appeared to be looking towards him!

This must be the original 'lovely young lady' of Whitewell, he thought.

Stuart was surprised when, as they came closer at the bottom of the stairs, Kristin spoke to her. They exchanged cheery 'Hello there, how are you?' type greetings and Stuart and Kristin went one way, 'the lovely young lady' another.

"Do you know that girl? Who is she?" Stuart was keen to know before they reached the car.

"Oh that's Laura-Lee. Laura-Lee Dillon," Kristin told him, trying to sound ever so matter-of-fact.

She had a good idea what was coming next.

# 3

# What's The World Coming To?

SHE DIDN'T HAVE to wait long to be proved right either.

They hadn't even made it home before Stuart asked, "You wouldn't have a phone number for that girl you were speaking to there would you, Kristin?"

"No, I don't but I'm sure I could get it for you if you were interested," young sister replied, with a twinkle in her eye.

Kristin did as she had promised and Stuart picked up the courage to phone Laura-Lee. "Hello there," he began, "this is Stuart Elliott, Kristin's brother. We saw you at 'Whitewell' one night if you remember?"

"Oh yes," came the soft reply. "I think I remember seeing you." Laura-Lee was doing her best to appear shy, or surprised, or both.

"Well I was wondering if you would like to meet me some night? Maybe go to the cinema or something?" Stuart had no small talk for this lovely girl that he had never even spoken to before. It was best, he reckoned, to go straight to the point.

There was a momentary silence on the line before Laura-Lee came back with, "I'm not sure about that now. I would have to think it over"

When further coaxing brought a similar non-committal response Stuart got the felling that this beautiful young girl was playing a game of 'hard-to-get' and so he opted to back off.

"That's OK, we will just leave it then," he said. "Maybe some other..." He didn't even have a chance to finish the sentence before Laura-Lee interrupted him. "No. But yes. I didn't mean to say No. It's all right. I don't want you to think that I don't want to go out or anything," she replied. It all sounded a bit garbled but what it meant was, yes I want to go out with you, and I have just been waiting for you to ring!

Stuart was pleased at this sudden confession by Laura-Lee and they arranged a date to meet. What his new girlfriend didn't know on their first night out was that Stuart didn't have very much money. He had only five pounds to spend on that first date and when he had paid their way into the cinema and bought some sweets to eat during the film he had very little left! He just prayed that this girl wouldn't expect to round off the evening by going out for a meal in some exclusive restaurant!

Laura-Lee wasn't that kind of girl, Stuart was delighted to discover. She was an attractive, quiet Christian young woman and as they saw each other more often they couldn't wait to see each other even more often. It didn't take them long to come to the conclusion that God wanted them to be together for the rest of their lives and Pastor Norman Hobson performed their wedding ceremony in Whitewell Metropolitan Tabernacle in 1997. It was an inexpressible joy for two young people who were so much in love to be united in marriage and an even greater thrill was in store for them. In May of the following year they were to become mum and dad to God's gift of a baby son, Nathan.

Stuart and his wife and little boy were living in Rathcoole on the outskirts of Belfast at that time and he took a job as a window-cleaner to help pay the bills. The young family then settled into an established pattern of life. They attended every possible meeting at Whitewell Metropolitan Tabernacle and Stuart, who had become a regular in the Glentoran first team, continued to play his football every weekend.

Towards the end of the 1999 – 2000 season Dave McParland, who was Director of Football at the Scottish Club, Motherwell, came over to Northern Ireland a few times to watch Stuart play. Billy Davis, the team manager, then came over to watch him in the last game of the season against Portadown. It was obvious that something had impressed them about the Irish League player who had caught the headlines a number of times for his goal-scoring ability.

When the season finished Stuart was named runner-up to Northern Ireland Player of the Year next to Vinny Arkins. He went away on holiday with Laura-Lee and Nathan in the early summer with the feeling that he had played his last game for

Glentoran. Towards the end of the holiday he started to feel the thought of the future lying heavily on his mind and began to pray for guidance. "Lord, if you want me to stay in the Irish League we can survive. I am still in my window-cleaning job and we can make it," was how he usually introduced the subject with his Heavenly Director of Life. This always came before the 'but-if' bit. It was the progression of the prayer and went on, "But if you have something else for me please show me Your way. I want to be in Your will for my life, whatever happens."

They hadn't been long home until God answered his prayer, and showed Stuart His way. He had a telephone call from Roy Coyle, the Glentoran manager, just a day or two before pre-season training was due to begin. What he had to say was what Stuart had been half-hoping for, as it would be his big break, but half-dreading, wondering if he would be able to cope with it. It was that Dave McParland and Billy Davis from Motherwell Football Club wanted to sign him. He was to meet the club representatives in the Park Avenue Hotel in Belfast on Sunday July 2 at 3.00 pm to discuss terms.

Stuart went to Whitewell as usual that Sunday morning but he didn't hear a lot of what the pastor was saying. He was in the church that he loved, surrounded by Christian people he loved, but he was lost in a world of his own. It was a world of prayer for guidance, a world of anticipation and trepidation.

The men from Motherwell had hired a special room for the meeting and after a general all-round introduction Roy Coyle and Dave McParland began discussing what they called 'the figures.' Meanwhile Stuart, whose future in football was the reason for the negotiations, sat listening in a state that bordered on disbelief.

Was this him they were talking about? Stuart Elliot who had spent half of his life trying to convince himself that he was a born loser. That he was never going to make it. That he always had been, and always would be, 'too small' for any and every challenge of life.

He was on a direct line to heaven, more in the thoughts running through his brain than in any words that he could form into an orderly, logical prayer. 'God help me here. I only want Your will,' was the unspoken burden of his heart.

The inferiority complex that had plagued Stuart since boyhood days came to the surface again at the shaking-hands stage of the afternoon with all the papers duly signed.

"Thank you very much," he said to Dave McParland. "I'll try my best to make it into the first team."

The Director of Football from Motherwell F.C. seemed a little surprised at this remark. "Son, I haven't come over here to sign you for the reserves!" he exclaimed. "You are one of our major signings for the season!"

Stuart Elliot walked out of that room feeling on top of the world. He was going to play 'across the water.' 'Thank You God. Thank You," he kept repeating in the car on the way back to Rathcoole.

When he arrived home and told Laura-Lee the exciting news she was very happy for him, and to go with him to Scotland, but they had a lot of planning to do. It had been agreed that Stuart would join his new club on Tuesday July 11, so they had just a little over a week to prepare themselves, physically, emotionally and spiritually for the move. Stuart began by telling his family, and then his friends at Whitewell Metropolitan Tabernacle, of his transfer. He had almost to keep pinching himself to make sure he was alive, and his dream had indeed come true, while talking to all these very supportive people. Next thing on the to-do list was handing in his notice to his window-cleaning job. None of the professional footballers he had met so far needed to clean windows to help make ends meet!

With all the 'ends tied up' as far as he could, Stuart decided to take his wife and little boy off on another short holiday. They would go up to Portrush for a couple of days to celebrate!

On Saturday, just three days before Stuart was due to start his professional career, Laura-Lee, Nathan and he went round the north coast from Portrush to the village of Ballintoy, and drove down the winding road to its scenic harbour. When there, Stuart left his wife and little son by the car and went for a walk along the pier, past the tiny boats with their colourful mirror-reflections in the still water, and out on to the rocks beyond. He just wanted to be on his own. There was so much to get sorted out in his mind.

Stuart walked on towards the sea until he ended up standing on a large rock gazing across to Rathlin Island and the faint outline of the Scottish coast in the heat haze beyond. When he realised that he was looking at the country to which he was taking his family, and in which he hoped to establish himself as a footballer, he was scared.

What did the future hold? Was he doing the right thing?

Standing there, with only a few squabbling seagulls for company, he prayed, "Lord, I'm pretty frightened about all of this. I want You to be the centre of my life and

I am asking you to lead me in Your will. I submit myself, and commit my family to You."

The following Tuesday Stuart and Laura-Lee left little Nathan with Laura-Lee's mum and travelled over to Motherwell. They were going to have to find somewhere to live. The young couple settled into the Moorings Hotel in the town for the night in preparation for a very busy day to follow.

First item on the programme for Wednesday was when Stuart had to sign his formal contract with the club. Next up was a trip out with Dave McParland to have a look at a house that he had thought Stuart and his wife might like to rent until they had the chance to look around for something to buy if they wished.

When they drove up into a lovely cul-de-sac in a quiet area of the town the couple were taken aback. Then when Dave invited them to 'Come on in and have a look around,' a beautiful four-bedroom house they were bowled over completely! Dave allowed them to walk through what to them was like a mansion out of a storybook, marvelling at every room and in the sheer space of the place, before asking, "Would you like this? "

Both of them were almost speechless but Stuart managed to say, with what he hoped was the composure of a professional, "Yes thanks, Dave. This will be fine!"

That was the high point of the day. The low point came when Laura-Lee had to return to Belfast and Nathan that night, and Stuart was left alone in the Moorings Hotel. He was to stay there and fulfil his commitments with his new club until arrangements could be made for his wife to bring their little boy over and they would be complete as a family once more.

Stuart attended the training sessions with his new club at their ground, Fir Park, Motherwell, and was enjoying it until something gave him a nasty shock. At the training session one day he had been given the fixture list for the new season and when he looked down it, back in his room at the hotel, he discovered something that gave him a jolt. It was something that he should have considered before leaving the Irish League, but hadn't.

This was Scotland, and Motherwell Football Club was scheduled to have seven Sunday fixtures!

Falling on his knees beside his bed Stuart began to cry out to God in prayer and anguish. He had already been missing the reassuring company of his wife and the warmth of the fellowship of his Christian friends back home. Now this!

"Oh God, I have made a big mistake here," he cried. "I have pledged to honour you with my life and here I am, under contract to play football on Your day! What have I done?! What should I do?!"

As he remained on his knees Stuart felt the peace of God take over in his heart. "It's all right my son,' his heavenly Father told him. "You are my child. I will look after you. 'The Sabbath was made for man, and not man for the Sabbath,' as my Word says. I am your Lord every day of the week. Put Me first as you have promised and everything will work out."

With that mini-crisis out of the way Stuart then soon had another landmark experience to face. It was his first league game for Motherwell, which happened to be a home match against Dundee.

It was a lovely sunny afternoon when Stuart drove up to Fir Park. He was a little apprehensive as he walked towards the dressing room. This was not only his first time to take the field in Motherwell's colours but it would also be his first to meet the whole team. Some of the squad had been away on a pre-season tour when Stuart arrived at the club and so he hadn't met them up until that moment.

Stuart was overawed as he looked around the dressing room when he had pushed in and found a spot to change. On one side there was Andy Goram, the former Rangers and Scotland goalkeeper, and along a couple of bodies from him was John Spencer who had once played for Chelsea. Down at the other end were Lee McCullough and Lee McMillan. These were all big, tall, broad men, excellent physical specimens. They looked to Stuart like contestants from 'The World's Strongest Man.'

There sitting among them, lacing up his boots and feeling scared out of his wits, was this raw young rookie from east Belfast. He had his head bent forward so nobody could see that he had his eyes closed as he whispered another of the panic-button prayers that had been his lifeline for the previous three weeks.

"O God, if You don't help me here I'm never going to get through this," he sighed, earnestly and inwardly.

Just after that John Spencer stood up, and reaching back into his bag he pulled out a statue of Buddha. Holding this up for everyone to see he announced, "I want everybody here to rub Buddha's head for luck."

Stuart trembled. He watched as a few players before him rubbed the head of the statue as John had suggested. The Buddha was coming his way.

When the towering figure of John Spencer leaned down towards Stuart he said, "Now son, it's your turn. Give Buddha's head a rub for luck."

"I'm sorry John, but I can't do that," Stuart said quietly.

John Spencer wasn't used to having anyone refuse him and reacted with a forceful, "You can't do that! Why can you not do that?!"

"I can't do that because I don't worship graven images," Stuart replied, with a confidence in his voice that could only have come in answer to his panic petition. "I serve another Master. I believe in God. I'm a born again Christian."

Grunting something like, "Oh it's like that is it," the man with the statue lifted his head and moved on, leaving Stuart to stand up, and then go out and try to play football on shaking legs.

Starting a new job anywhere can be quite a challenging experience for anyone but for the young man from Belfast making his debut 'across the water' in front of a crowd of eager, and often vociferous fans, it was a nightmare. He felt he didn't play as well as he could have and Motherwell lost the match by two goals to nil.

On the way back to Belfast in the plane that evening he was down in the dumps. There was only one solution and that was to talk it over with his Head Coach. "God I can't do this," he felt he had to admit. "I'm out of my depth in this league. The level of football is far too quick for me."

"Don't worry about it, Stuart. Just trust me. You are good enough and you can make it at that level, trust Me. I have brought you there, and I will look after you there." was the reply he received from his Heavenly Headquarters.

Stuart's purpose in returning to Northern Ireland was to bring Laura-Lee and Nathan back with him on the ferry, and when the family had settled into the house in the cul-de-sac, husband and father felt much better. His football improved too and in one of the next matches for Motherwell against Kilmarnock he scored two goals. Soon the other members of the team were inviting him out for a drink with them, and as it had been with Glentoran, so it was with Motherwell. He declined, preferring to be at home with his 'wife and the kid.'

By mid-September his season had taken off and that was when Billy Davis arrived into the dressing room one morning as the lads were preparing for training. He was holding a letter.

He stepped across to Stuart, and handing it over to him said, "Here Stuart, this one's for you."

As Stuart reached for it, a bit bewildered as to who would be writing to him at Motherwell Football Club, Billy went on to remark with a laugh, "What's the world coming to?"

# 4

# I'm Starting You Tomorrow

BILLY OBVIOUSLY KNEW who the letter was from and what it was about. Stuart didn't though. He hadn't been expecting it.

It was from Sammy McIlroy, the Northern Ireland team coach, telling Stuart that he had been selected to play for his country in their next match. This was against Malta and was to be played in Windsor Park Belfast in a few weeks time.

Stuart's teammates congratulated him on his call-up. It was a big honour for the 'too-small' boy from east Belfast who thought he was never going to make it into the big time. Now he was holding a letter telling him when to meet for training with his national team!

Meeting up with established members of the Northern Ireland team like Jim Magilton and Neil Lennon in the Stormont Hotel was another new experience for Stuart. Now he didn't have to look up to these men with the same level of awe as once he did. Not that they had changed, but he had! Stuart Elliot could possibly end up playing alongside them on the same team!

His international career didn't start all that well. Stuart was so tired with nervous exhaustion that he slept in the first morning and was last to join the team bus to go training! The senior members of the squad treated it as a joke. The new boy on the block had better sharpen up!

Stuart was treated to a pleasant surprise that night in the hotel. He discovered that John Bevere, from the Christian organisation Messenger International, was speaking at a meeting in one of the public rooms. He could hardly believe it! Stuart went to it and sat, in his first Northern Ireland squad shirt, listening to the renowned writer and Bible teacher conduct a seminar on effective Christian living.

There was yet another pleasant surprise to come his way the following evening too when he met Sammy McIlroy in a hotel corridor. It was the Friday night before the game and the boss had a message for Stuart. The young Motherwell player couldn't believe that just a few words could make his heart thump like those few words did. They were "I'm starting you tomorrow, Stuart."

Stepping out on to the turf at the Oval for Glentoran for the first time had been a wonderful experience for Stuart but it didn't even compare with this! Stepping out on to the turf in a packed out Windsor Park, Belfast, for his international debut against Malta on Saturday September 2, 2000, was something else!

The flags were fluttering in the breeze high above the stands, which were packed with fans in good voice. Laura-Lee and little Nathan plus as many other members of Stuart's family as were interested in football were all there, among the huge crowd somewhere, to support him.

It was the proudest moment of his career to date. Is this real? he thought as he lined up with the men he had tried to emulate for years, to represent his country.

The teams fanned out across the pitch with each man taking up a starting position, and the whistle blew. There could be no doubting the reality of the situation now. This was the real thing. This was down to business. This was what Stuart Elliott had been dreaming of walking down the Newtownards Road on his way home from his first trial match for Belfast Primary Schools.

Stuart soon settled into the pattern of play, up yet another level, and had a good game. Phil Gray scored the only goal in the match to secure a Northern Ireland victory and Stuart was pleased to finish his first international on the winning side. He also hoped that he had done enough to keep his place in the team.

When he returned to Motherwell, Stuart had to turn his mind to family as well as football matters. The house they had been so pleased with when they saw it at first had been rented for six months to allow Laura-Lee and him to make their own selection of somewhere more permanent to live. Now it was decision time.

Their choice of location was influenced by two factors. It had to be close enough to Motherwell for Stuart to attend for training and matches but it would be a bonus if it were also to be within easy reach of Falkirk. This was vital to Stuart and Laura-Lee who had already been attending a Whitewell Metropolitan Church extension in that Scottish town. They found Pastor George McKimm, from the People's Church, and also originally from Belfast, to be a dynamic preacher. After visiting a number of properties on the market they decided to buy a house in Cumbernauld, which was between Motherwell and Falkirk. This would allow Stuart access to the two main features in his life as well as his family. These were his church and his club.

Stuart hadn't been long in the People's Church until he started being invited to speak at a number of Youth Groups around the district. Youth leaders had heard of this 'new player at Motherwell' who was a Christian, and asked him along to speak to their members, knowing that the boys in the group particularly would be keen to hear what he had to say.

When the first invitations came in, some directly and some through Pastor McKimm, Stuart baulked at the idea. 'Lord, I can't do that kind of thing. I'm not cut out for public speaking. I'm a footballer, not a preacher,' was his initial reaction. His ingrained inferiority complex, his 'who am I?' sense of inadequacy, was raising its unwelcome head again.

God had a message for him, however. It was basically that he could, and as His servant he would. 'I have brought you here for a purpose,' was God's unequivocal response to Stuart's reservations about unfitness. 'You asked me to lead you into My will for your life. This is it. Go out and tell those young people what I have done for you and what I can do for them.'

The challenge was great but the command was clear and Stuart began to become actively involved in Christian work, both in the People's Church and local youth groups. It was in The People's Church also that Stuart had a special spiritual experience.

He and Laura-Lee were sitting up at the front of the church listening to George Millar, a visiting Bible teacher one evening when the speaker stopped in the middle of his address. Pointing down towards where Stuart was sitting he called out, "Come up here young man."

Stuart looked around, confused. Was it him the preacher meant or was there somebody behind him? He had just turned round to glance back when the voice from the platform put the matter beyond any doubt. "Yes, it's you I mean. You with the purple tie on. And is that your wife beside you? Bring her too."

The couple looked at each other wondering what to do. They felt a bit embarrassed. How could they rise and go up onto the platform in front of the whole congregation?

An urgent "Yes, it's you. Come on," from the speaker helped ease them into action. Rising from their seat Stuart and Laura-Lee began walking shyly up to where the preacher was standing. While they were on their way up he spoke across to Pastor McKimm, asking him to bring some anointing oil.

When husband and wife made it to the preacher's side he announced, "Young man, I believe that God's hand is upon your life. I want to anoint you with oil in His name." Taking the oil from the church pastor he proceeded to do as he said he felt God telling him to do, and anointed Stuart with it before the packed congregation.

As he continued to command a first team place with Motherwell, Stuart also became a regular in the Northern Ireland squad. If there could possibly be yet another high point in his career it would come when he scored his first goal for his country. With the way Stuart was playing it would only be a matter of time until this happened. It came in an away game against Bulgaria in a World Cup qualifier on Saturday March 28, 2001.

Northern Ireland were three goals down when Stuart rose above the goalkeeper to head a high ball into the net. It was a special feeling to hear the cheers of the small posse of travelling fans and to have scored his opening international goal. A penalty was awarded and Northern Ireland scored from it to set up a hectic, but ultimately unsuccessful onslaught on the Bulgarian goal in search of a draw.

Another proud moment came for Stuart in the return leg of that fixture on the first Saturday in June, when Bulgaria came to play his team at Windsor Park. There was the usual exuberant crowd of spectators present and the greatest player ever to play for Northern Ireland, George Best, was a member of the TV commentary team. Stuart felt that he had done himself justice that day, and was awarded an unexpected accolade. George Best, in his review of the game, as the players were making their way to the dressing room and the spectators were streaming out of the ground, said, "Stuart Elliot was my Man of the Match." Stuart considered that high praise indeed.

Having become more involved in outreach evangelism with the People's Church in Falkirk, Stuart had a conviction that grew in his mind week by week. It was that he should arrange something to try and bring the Gospel to the people in the town where he played his football, Motherwell.

He began by approaching three men who were leaders in different churches in the town, and one of them was also the co-ordinator of Youth For Christ in Scotland. Stuart explained the vision he had to hire the Motherwell football ground, Fir Park, for a night and invite a number of well-known Christian sports personalities along to speak. The three men liked this innovative idea as a means of taking the message to the people and offered to sponsor such a venture.

With that kind of enthusiastic backing, Stuart's next step was to approach the club managers to ask if he could possibly rent the ground for an evening in early June 2002. They were very helpful and agreed to take only one quarter of the total ticket sales for the event as their fee for the use of the stadium.

Now that Stuart had been assured of financial and spiritual backing, as well as the venue for the outreach event he was planning, the next step was to contact speakers. He asked others to join him in prayer for guidance as he invited a number of high-profile Christian sportsmen to take part.

Stuart began making all the necessary arrangements for what he and others had hoped would be a night of blessing to many, with prayerful zeal. The day before the event he was greatly discouraged, however, to discover that of the 2000 tickets he had printed for the event, only 400 had been sold.

'What's going on here, God?' Stuart prayed as he walked around the streets of Motherwell that night. He couldn't rest or relax at home. It was important to him to 'wrestle with God' to try and find out why so few appeared interested in what he had prayed would be remembered as a significant spiritual landmark in the Lanarkshire town. He ended up by committing the entire event into the all-powerful hands of his Heavenly Father, asking Him to meet every need.

When the next evening came Stuart thought that this must just have been a hare-brained idea of his. He must have got it wrong again. An hour before the stadium outreach was due to start there was an intense thunderstorm over Motherwell. Lightning flashed across the sky, the thunder rolled and boomed overhead and torrents of rain poured down.

What have I done? Stuart wondered. Is God angry with me? Nobody will come out on a night like this!

He was totally wrong to think that, though. About fifteen minutes before the scheduled start time the rain stopped and the sky cleared but only about a hundred hardy souls had made it into Fir Park. Then they started to come. And come. And come. Bus after bus, from all over Scotland it seemed, drew up outside the ground and disgorged their contents. The people were flocking in, and by the time Stuart stood up to welcome everybody there were about 1500 in the stands!

What a relief! How Stuart thanked God as he saw the size of the crowd, all eager to hear the sportsmen speak. Among those telling about their work, and witnessing to their faith were Eric Boyers, the chaplain to Manchester United, Steve Connors from the Chicago Bears and Mike McCurrie, a FIFA referee.

Stuart brought the closing message of the evening from a Bible verse. It was Ecclesiastes chapter 11 and verse 9. 'Rejoice, O young man in your youth, and let your heart cheer you in the days of your youth… But know that for all these things God will bring you into judgement.'

He went on to remind the large crowd that everybody has a variety of choices to make every day in life, but some are more important than others. He referred to the choice Moses made to serve God when he could have ended up with a wealthy lifestyle as a prince in Egypt, and the choice Jesus made to go willingly to the cross to die for our sins when He could easily have avoided it.

The final challenge of the evening, he said, was the ultimate choice of 'What will you do with Jesus?' Stuart then closed his short message by making an appeal for any who were interested in becoming Christians to come forward. Many did and were counselled, with most of them committing their lives to the Lord Jesus.

It was an awesome night, but it still wasn't over.

On the way back to Cumbernauld in the car Stuart was thanking God for all that had happened that evening and praying for guidance in the future when he felt a powerful shudder pass through his body. It was scary at first but Stuart believed that it could only have been the power of God answering his prayer and adding the divine stamp of approval to his preaching that night. It represented a reaffirmation of the lesson he had just learnt. Stuart Elliott could be a footballer and a preacher.

Where did he go from here?

What had God in store for him now?

During the long June days Stuart became first gradually, and then firmly, convinced of one thing. Whatever it was, or wherever it was, it wouldn't be in Motherwell, Cumbernauld or Falkirk.

He began walking around the inside of the deserted Fir Park stadium, praying.

"Lord I feel in my heart that my time here is rapidly coming to an end," he would begin. This was followed by, "If it is Your will for me to move on please show me where it is You want me to go now."

Although he had often heard in meetings that 'God works out His purposes in His own time and way,' Stuart was often tempted to add another short question to his sincere petition.

It was, "And Lord, if You don't mind, could You make it soon?"

# 5

# What Did I Tell You?

THE LORD ANSWERED his prayer, in both the spoken petition and the unvoiced condition. God showed Stuart His will for his future, and He did it 'soon.'

It was early July and the Motherwell team had returned to Fir Park for pre-season training. On the third day back, Terry Butcher, who had replaced Billy Davis as the club manager, asked Stuart to see him in his office.

He hadn't been long in before Terry told him the news he had been praying to hear, but when he heard it in so many words it came as a bit of a jolt. "Hull City have been on with us over the last couple of days," he began. "They are keen to sign you, Stuart. We have agreed terms with them and now it's up to you."

Stuart told him that he would have to think about it for it would mean moving not only himself but also his wife and little son. There was also the matter of personal terms to be agreed, but he promised to let the manager know of his decision 'in a day or two.'

He told Laura-lee of Hull's interest in him when he arrived home and they both agreed that they would 'pray about it.' Stuart had been praying for something like this to happen, and now he felt he ought to pray more about it. It would be a big change for all three of them, and yet if it were God's signal to move on, he didn't want to ignore it.

Later that evening Stuart was sitting in the study where he loved to lose himself in the Scriptures at every opportunity. He was working on pages of figures but they weren't from Numbers. It was tempting to look for 'an attractive package' but in the middle of it all Stuart would draw himself up and remember that he had pledged himself repeatedly to go where God wanted him. Would he be brave enough to do that whatever the circumstances?

Stuart was still attempting to balance his spiritual and practical books when the phone rang. It was Terry Butcher again. "Sorry to seem to be putting pressure on you, Stuart," he said," but Hull have been on the phone again. They want to know your decision tomorrow. They are keen to have everything settled up as soon as possible."

"Right, Terry," Stuart replied. "I'll let you, and them, know one way or the other, in the morning."

The man in demand spent a few more hours in serious consideration and earnest prayer and although he didn't like to feel pressurised it was probably a good thing. He was going to have to make up his mind within the next twelve hours.

It was almost midnight when he went in to speak to his wife who had already retired to bed. "I have decided to make the move to Hull City, Laura," he said, "if that's OK with you. I believe this is God's will for us. Just think, of all the clubs in England or Scotland that could have shown an interest in signing me, the only one to come up with an offer is Hull City. And do you realise that Hull is one of the few places over on this side of the water that has a 'Whitewell' extension church, as well as Falkirk? I know it will be a big break for us, but I believe that this is of God."

"If it's what you feel we ought to do Stuart, I'll be quite happy to go with you. I have always told you that," Laura-lee assured him without hesitation.

Shortly after informing Terry of his decision the following morning the wheels whirred into motion very quickly. Stuart had a phone call later that day from Adam Pearson, the chairman of Hull City Football Club, arranging for him to come down to the east Yorkshire city and discuss personal terms and sign a contract.

On July 11, 2002, the family of three, dad the footballer, Laura-lee the footballer's wife, and Nathan their little son were flown south to Hull in a private jet. They were then met by the manager's chauffeur-driven car and driven to the Ramada-Jarvis Hotel where the talks and signing were to take place.

The Hull management team had booked a special room for the occasion and after they had finalised the negotiations Adam Pearson and Jan Molby, the first team coach, presented their new player to the press. They seemed pleased to have acquired the signature of Stuart Elliot to strengthen their squad at Hull City AFC.

After the signing Adam Pearson took the family out to see where Stuart would be starting his playing career at the club, and then on to where he would be continuing it. The old ground at Boothferry Park had been in need of renovation for some time so it had been sold and the club was building a completely new-state-of-the-art stadium just up the road. Stuart was taken aback when he walked out on to what would some day be a football pitch and not a construction site. Adam Pearson told him that this new KC Stadium as it was to be known, was costing £45million to build and would be equipped with every modern facility.

Stuart was happy as he accompanied his wife and little son back to Scotland to make arrangements for the move south to Yorkshire. Their house in Cumbernauld was put on the market and sold very quickly. This, to Stuart, was another sign that he had been wise to agree to the transfer.

Perhaps the hardest part of leaving Scotland was saying goodbye to Pastor George McKimm and their friends at The People's Church in Falkirk. Stuart had matured so much in his Christian faith while there and he and Laura-Lee would miss the friends they had made in the fellowship. Yet Stuart felt that God was leading him on to help expand the outreach and witness of the church in Hull.

Although events moved rapidly that summer Stuart hadn't everything quite settled before it was time for him to travel down to Hull to start playing the pre-season 'friendlies' with his new club. This meant that Laura-Lee was left to tidy up the 'odds and ends' while he stayed in a hotel and looked out for somewhere for the three of them to live.

It seemed as though the Lord was opening up the way for them again for Stuart learnt of a lovely property to rent, went to see it, consulted Laura-Lee about it, and took it. Soon they were together as a family again and Stuart began his career at Hull City Football Club well. He chose to demonstrate the skill of his 'sweet left foot,' by scoring seven goals in the pre-season warm-up games.

They had only been in their rented home in Yorkshire a matter of weeks when Stuart and Laura-Lee had a different kind of experience. Nathan was due to start school. They enquired around to find out which was their local school and they both left him there on his first day, and then wept silently on the way back home in the car. This was another emotional milestone passed for them, and it happened within weeks of the upset of moving house.

They were to discover later that they were the only members of the family annoyed. Nathan had been quite happy in school all day!

On his first home league game of the season Stuart continued where he had left off at the end of pre-season, by scoring for Hull against Southend United. Although Stuart felt encouraged by his personal performances in the opening games the overall team results did not live up to the expectations of management, and Jan Molby was forced to leave by early October.

It was a critical point for the club. They had spent money on new players, they were on schedule to be opening a brand new stadium at Christmas and they were in the bottom half of the bottom half of the league.

After Jan had left and before the new manager, Peter Taylor arrived, Stuart was speaking to Adam Pearson one day. The chairman seemed at a loss to know what to do to turn around a depressing-looking situation at Hull City AFC. Stuart's simple message to him was, "I believe that God Almighty will do wonderful things at this club. I'm quite sure that He has led me here but I don't want you to think that I am saying that I am going to turn everything around on my own. I'm not. I'm only one player, but I'm convinced that God has something big in store for us."

The chairman wasn't quite sure what to make of this positive prediction. He had never imagined that God Almighty was the slightest bit concerned about league football, and so he shrugged his shoulders, smiled benignly and grunted, " I hope you're right, Stuart. How I just hope you are right!"

Sunderland, which at that time was a Premiership football club, came down to Hull and played the hosts in a friendly game to mark the opening of the new KC Stadium, just before Christmas. This huge celebration, with a packed out ground and a fireworks display marked the start of a run of better results for Hull.

As he began to settle down in Yorkshire Stuart found himself in a situation where his circumstances were changing, and it seemed all for the better, at a breath-taking rate.

He had told Pastor John Thompson from the Living Hope Church soon after he arrived in Hull that he was there 'for the long term' and that he would be keen to help in any way he could to see people reached for Christ and the church witness developed. Stuart was standing with the pastor one day in the spring of 2003, on yet another construction site. It was in the windowless shell of what was to be a new building for the church, which had long since outgrown the accommodation it was using at the time.

"I'm beginning to feel a bit like Nehemiah, John," he quipped. "No matter where I have gone, or where I go to, down here, somebody is building something and I am stuck in the middle of it"

The pastor smiled and enquired, "What do you mean, Stuart?"

Stuart had no difficulty reeling off an answer to that one. "Well when I first arrived at Hull Football Club they were still building their new stadium, and now Peter is trying to build a successful team. Here we are in what will be a lovely new church, which we pray will be used for God's glory. When I leave you I will be going over to our new house, which is almost complete to talk to the builders about some fixtures and fittings. And the best thing of all is that Laura-Lee is expecting again. We are building our family, too."

"I see what you mean, it's all very exciting for you Stuart," Pastor Thompson replied, happy for him and glad to have a committed and enthusiastic Christian like him in his congregation.

It was indeed exciting. Everything seemed to be advancing at once. Stuart loved it, and would constantly burst out in praise to God in odd moments at any time of the day. "Thank You God!" he would exclaim. "Thank You Lord for your goodness to us!"

On Tuesday July 1, 2003, Pastor James McConnell of Whitewell Metropolitan Tabernacle, Belfast, came across to speak at the official opening of the Living Hope Church in Hull. Local dignitaries, people from the surrounding area and the resident congregation all packed into the new building for the event. That was to prove a momentous day in the life of the expanding fellowship for a number were saved during and after the ceremony and were soon to join the church.

A few weeks later, on August 3, Stuart experienced the joy and privilege of fatherhood for the second time. Nathan now had a baby sister and his mum and dad were delighted to welcome their little daughter, Hannah-Grace into the family they were building. They looked on her as a precious gift from God, and vowed, as they had done with Nathan, to give her the best possible start in life. This, they were well aware, meant bringing her up in an atmosphere where she would be surrounded by loving care and constant prayer.

The following year was one of helping care for the family and becoming more active in the life of the church, which was conducting a series of different programmes to reach out into the local community with the Gospel. It was a time of laying the foundations for, and then cementing, lasting relationships both in the family and community, rather than becoming involved in bricks-and-mortar building.

Stuart had a good year at the club, too, and at the end of the season Hull City AFC finished second in League Two and were promoted to League One. It was nearly two years on from when Stuart told the chairman that great things were in store for the club. He, though, saw this promotion as merely a stepping-stone and not the final destination. Stuart reckoned that with the squad of players they had, and the way they were playing, they could go higher still.

At the beginning of the 2004 –2005 season, when Hull City were about to start their campaign in League One, where they would no doubt encounter a different level of opposition, Stuart was reading his Bible in a hotel room in London. He had been studying the Minor Prophets and that evening was concentrating on the prayer of Habakkuk in the final chapter of that short prophecy. That was when he was struck by the opening words of the final verse. As he read, ' The Lord God is my strength, and He will make my feet like hinds' feet,' he took them as a promise from God and turned them into a prayer.

"Lord, let me honour You with my feet, and all of my life, this season," was his humble petition.

For a Christian footballer, praying is an important start to any match or season, but playing is the part managers and fans want to see. And before Christmas that year Hull City were riding high in League One and Stuart had scored 20 goals. It was a dream start to the year. Other clubs, both in the Championship and the Premiership were beginning to show an interest in this prolific striker, the 'too-small-to-make-it' boy from Belfast, the winger with the 'sweet left foot.'

When all was going well, and Hull City were beginning to have other clubs in contact about Stuart, what appeared like a catastrophe occurred. During the match against Huddersfield on New Year's Day, 2005, Stuart was elbowed in the face by another player and sustained a fractured cheekbone.

The transfer window was about to close, Stuart was sidelined for a possible eight weeks, and the interest in him, which had been mounting gradually over the previous two months disappeared overnight. It was like a beautiful sandcastle that had taken a family of excited children an entire afternoon to decorate. When the tide came creeping up the beach it disappeared without trace. The sand was completely flat again.

Friends who had been following the rising star's career with interest and scouts and managers from some other senior clubs saw Stuart's broken cheekbone as an unexpected and unwanted hindrance to further negotiations about his future.

At the beginning he saw it that way too. Was he never set to make it to the Premiership? Had his chance gone, all because of an elbow in the face?

As he began to reflect on his situation and continued to reach out to others through Living Hope that January, however, Stuart realised that his overall Manager of Football wasn't in the KC Stadium in Hull. He just happened to have his Headquarters in heaven, and that was where Stuart was being directed from, by a powerful, invisible Hand.

When he recognised his injury as being nothing more than a temporary setback to his advancing career, in order to allow him to remain in Hull, where he was being afforded endless opportunities to make mighty advances for the Kingdom of God, Stuart was quite happy. He submitted to the situation and when his cheekbone healed sufficiently he was back in his 'Tigers' shirt, scoring yet more goals.

Hull City AFC had a remarkable season and by May 2005, Stuart had scored 29 goals making him the highest scorer in the League and the team were runners-up in League One. Automatic promotion to the Championship and another challenge in a totally different, and potentially more remunerative, level of football lay ahead. This caused massive excitement in the city and even resulted in the team being invited to take part in a city tour in an open-top bus to show the promotion trophy to their loyal fans.

May 8 was a big night in the city. Thousands of cheering fans lined the streets as the bus made its way to the City Hall, and many of them wanted to wave to their goal-scoring hero, Stuart.

About an hour later, as the team were standing on the balcony of the City Hall, waving to the still cheering crowds all adorned in club shirts and scarves, Stuart turned to the chairman who was standing right beside him

"What did I tell you Adam?" he asked, his face glowing with the excitement of the occasion. "Remember what I said about God Almighty going to do something marvellous for us? What about this?"

"Yes, Stuart, I remember," he conceded. "I said that I hoped you were right. It looks as though you were."

# 6

# Scoring Goals, Winning Souls

IT IS VITAL that professional footballers maintain themselves in a state of peak physical fitness and excellent general health to give value for money for every minute they are on the pitch. What happens though if they are expected to perform to the optimum of their highly-prized ability when feeling 'a bit under the weather?'

Stuart found that out in one of Northern Ireland's opening games in the World Cup qualifiers in October 2004. The match was away to Azerbaijan and Stuart, who was playing well for his club, was pleased to be awarded another cap for his country, but he found the going tough. He had felt queasy before the game and as it progressed his legs began weakening and he couldn't chase up every ball, as he would have liked.

On returning to the team hotel, and the room he was sharing with Aaron Hughes, after the match, he was violently sick and had to lie down. Stuart knew that he hadn't played as well as he could have, or should have, in what ended up as an unexciting scoreless draw. He had let both himself and his team down, and his big worry was that his lacklustre performance, which must have ranked amongst the worst of his international career to date, would influence the manager when it came to selecting the team for the next match. It was against Austria at Windsor Park, Belfast, in four days time.

When the manager named his team for the match in Windsor Park, Stuart was disappointed, but not surprised to find that he was 'on the bench.' Recognising that this was entirely predictable, he committed the situation to God and prayer, asking for grace and guidance.

On the way down into the city for the match from the team hotel in the County Antrim countryside Stuart was sitting reading his Bible in the coach. He had turned to 1 Samuel chapter 17 about David and Goliath and as he pondered the story it dawned on him that young David had spent all his early life 'on the sidelines.' He had been forced to live in the shadow of older, stronger brothers until God called him into action.

Could something like that be going to happen to him that night?

It was well into the second half and Austria was leading Northern Ireland by three goals to two when Stuart turned to Stephen Craigan who was sitting beside him.

"Wait to you see what's going to happen here, Stevie," he said with an uncanny confidence. "I'm going to go on and score the equaliser."

Stephen shook his head in disbelief, "How do you know that?" he asked.

"Just you wait and see," Stuart told him.

Five minutes later the manager made a substitution and Stuart was sent on to the pitch. It was then only a matter of minutes after that until a ball came back across the penalty box to Stuart and he hammered it into the goal at the kop end of Windsor Park. Northern Ireland had equalised, and Stuart had predicted that he would score the third goal!

When the match was over Stephen Craigan came across to Stuart, with a puzzled expression on his face, "That was great Stuart, but how did you know you were going to score?"

"You'll hardly believe me, Stevie, when I tell you, " Stuart began to explain, "But I'm sure God told me."

Another of the matches in that group was against England at Old Trafford, Manchester, and Northern Ireland were beaten 4 – 0. As Stuart walked off the pitch in the 'Theatre of Dreams' he was sorry that they had lost the match but he had John Terry's shirt slung across his shoulders. He had come a long way from the trembling ten-year old at the trial match in Strandtown Primary School, Belfast.

At the start of the autumn matches, Northern Ireland played Azerbaijan at Windsor Park and Stuart scored from a free kick. A penalty for Northern Ireland in the dying minutes of the game confirmed the victory for the home side. Stuart's goal raised his profile with the fans and when the programme for the match everybody was waiting for, the clash with England in Belfast, was produced, there was an action picture of Stuart on the cover.

Wednesday September 7, 2005 was the night that none of the 14,000 fans that packed into Windsor Park will ever forget. The only goal of the match from David Healey secured victory for the definite underdogs and sent the crowd wild with delight. This unexpected defeat of the star-studded English team sent shock waves reverberating through the world of football for days.

It was a night that Stuart will never forget either, but for a different reason. This was the fired up attitude of the Northern Ireland team. They were stung by the lack of press coverage in relation to them. Nearly all the reporting seemed to focus on the fact that the mighty English were coming to town. Stuart found himself praying before he left the hotel, "O God, some of these men are being worshipped like heroes, like idols, like gods even. Help me, and our team to be very aware that You are in control of this earth. This will have to be another David and Goliath job, but Lord You did it before and You can do it again."

The win over England lifted the team's spirits and increased expectations amongst Northern Ireland fans but these were to be dashed in the later matches. Defeats in October by Wales and then Austria were to see Northern Ireland drop down the league table and out of contention for a World Cup place.

Although Stuart enjoys his football, both for his club, Hull City AFC, and Northern Ireland it is not the sole, or main, motivating influence in his life. This is living for God and seeing other people come to faith in Christ and discover the joy and peace that he has found in knowing and living for Him.

Stuart is heavily involved with the church witness in Living Hope. He is on the leadership team and often leads the worship during the Sunday services when at home. His greatest joy, though, is to preach the good news of Jesus and His love. Over the past two years, as well as playing football at both club and international level, Stuart has been preaching in the Sunday evening evangelistic service in Living Hope to audiences of well over one hundred people.

Scoring a goal for a team is one kind of thrill and is apt to set Stuart dashing off in circles waving his arms in the air. Seeing a soul won for Christ is something different entirely. It sees him humbled in spirit, but joyful to the point of tears.

A goal scored will be recorded in a league table and posted on a team website. A soul saved will cause rejoicing in heaven and a new entry in the Lamb's Book of Life.

A goal scored is an earthly statistic.

A soul saved is an eternal investment.

That is why Stuart is so overjoyed to see people like young men and women come to the Saviour.

Jonathan was a quiet young man in his twenties. He had been coming to the church every Sunday evening for some time but showed no visible signs of interest in anything that was going on.

One night, though, Stuart was preaching and took as the theme of his address, Paul's sermon on Mars Hill in Athens, based on the Bible story in Acts 17. Towards the end of his message he drew attention to the different reactions of the hearers to Paul's presentation of Jesus and His resurrection.

"Some mocked," he pointed out, "another group put off making any decision, saying they would hear him again sometime. You will also notice that there were a few who believed, and their names are given here for the record." He then went on to challenge his congregation as to what they were 'going to do with Jesus,' that night. Would they laugh at Him, put off doing anything about Him until some other time, which may never come, or believe on Him that night?

It was a challenging message and at the end of it Stuart made an appeal but no one responded. He concluded his remarks by saying, 'Dionysius and Damaris may not have come to Jesus there and then when Paul preached on Mar's Hill. It could have been afterwards. The important thing is that they came. And the important thing is that you come to Him soon too. It's not too late if the Spirit of God is speaking to you."

The meeting was over and Stuart was walking down the aisle towards the door after the service when Jonathan came across to him. "Can I speak to you, Stuart?" he enquired.

"Of course you can," Stuart replied. "How can I help you?" He hoped he knew the answer to his own question and was not disappointed when it came.

"I just want to get right with God," was exactly the response Stuart had been waiting to hear.

"Come on out and let's sit in my car where we can have a chat about it, Jonathan," Stuart suggested and they hadn't been long out there until Jonathan had accepted Jesus as his Saviour.

Just before he left Stuart the new convert confessed, "You know I have been wanting to give my heart to Jesus for a while now but I could never pick up the courage to say to anybody. After you spoke tonight, though, I just had to do it."

Another evening Stuart told his congregation that he was going to speak to them about 'a subject too hot to handle.' It was with a great burden on his heart, he said, that he felt God was telling him to warn the people in his church about the dangers of rejecting Christ in life and spending eternity in hell as a result.

An awesome silence fell over the audience as he preached that evening. After the meeting, Helen, a young woman who had been coming along to the evening services with her mum for years, became a Christian. This caused great joy in the church and in her family, and there were further scenes of rejoicing a few months later when Helen was baptised.

Since the large rally in Fir Park, Motherwell, Stuart has been invited to speak at a number of meetings in football grounds. This allows him to combine two of his main interests in life. He is respected as a footballer, but anxious that others should also know about his faith.

Two recent visits to Scottish grounds proved pleasing to Stuart, as one was to provide the proof of the value of the other.

The first of these trips north of the border was to Airdrie Football ground, early in 2006. Stuart's friend, Brian Lowry helps run a group called Making A Difference, or MAD for short. The aim of this organisation is to show people from all kinds of backgrounds that Jesus really can make a difference in their lives.

When he arrived at Airdrie's ground Stuart found that a large crowd of men had gathered in one of the club's function rooms and were having a light meal. It struck him that this was a tremendous opportunity and a big responsibility. These men had come there for one reason. They were there to hear what Stuart Elliott, who used to play for rivals Motherwell, had to say.

After the meal Stuart introduced himself by telling the men a little about his football and the different clubs he had played for. The main thrust of what he had to say in that opening section of the evening however was about how he had committed his life to Christ as a young lad in Belfast and what that had meant to him in his career.

There then followed a question and answer session where the audience were invited to ask Stuart anything they liked and the questions that came were mostly about football. Brian had asked Stuart to prepare a short closing message for the men and to do this he chose a short statement from Isaiah chapter 53.

'Yet in pleased the Lord to bruise Him,' he read.

"Why would it please God to bruise his Son?" Stuart asked. "Surely a lot of us here today are fathers and we wouldn't dream of hurting our sons. We only want the best for them. What can this be all about?"

There were three reasons why God considered it necessary to 'bruise' His Son, Stuart told his audience in answer to the question he had posed. The first of these was that we are all sinners and in order for God to forgive us our sins someone had to take the punishment for them. That person was Jesus, the sinless Son of God.

The other two reasons why Jesus should have to die on the cross were to do with life now and in the future. Stuart explained that God wanted people to have Him with them and enjoy life to the full when living on earth. Then He planned to accept them into the home He had prepared for them in heaven when they died. It was only people who knew their sins forgiven could enter that holy habitation of God.

It was a very pointed and powerful twenty-minute presentation and while he was speaking Stuart could see that some of the men were drinking it all in as though they had never heard anything like it before. When the meeting was over a man came asking to 'have a word with' Stuart. "I'm Duncan," he said simply, "And I would like to give myself to God."

When they had found a quiet place to have a chat Stuart discovered that Duncan was a broken man. His background was littered with all kinds of complex issues yet all he wanted to do that night had been expressed in one sincere sentence. 'I would like to give myself to God.'

Stuart had never found people with that sort of deep determination hard to counsel and it wasn't long until Duncan had trusted Christ for salvation. It wasn't only Duncan, Stuart and the angels in heaven that were overjoyed that night either.

As Brian was saying goodbye to Stuart later on he said, "Duncan is my brother-in-law you know, and we have been praying for him for years. What has happened tonight is a tremendous answer to prayer."

It was almost a year later when Stuart was back in Scotland, and again at Brian's invitation. Encouraged by the spiritual blessing of the previous year's venture in Airdrie, he had asked Stuart to 'come up' to Hamilton to the Academicals football ground to do something similar.

When Stuart arrived at the venue he was looking around for Brian when another man spoke to him in a very friendly way, obviously glad to see him. Stuart replied with a cheery, "Hello there, how are you?" and resumed his search.

Within a matter of minutes he had found the man he was looking for. Stuart and he had only started to discuss the arrangements for the evening when Brian noticed the man who seemed to have been shadowing the visiting speaker-to-be. Stuart had a feeling that he was following him too, but was totally surprised and very embarrassed when Brian asked, "Are you not saying hello to Duncan?"

Stuart could barely believe it! Was this the same man? It certainly didn't look like the man he had spoken to a year or so before. That man had been dull and depressed, his face lined with worry and concern. This man was bright and happy and his face was shining!

"Hello Duncan, and sorry! I didn't even recognise you there," Stuart confessed. "You have changed completely!"

"Yes. You're right, Stuart," Duncan replied with a broad smile. "God has worked a wonderful thing in my life."

Stuart shook his hand warmly. "I'm thrilled to see you and hear that," he said.

Over the past two years Stuart's life story has been reaching out to an even larger audience, also. Whitewell Metropolitan Tabernacle produced his testimony on DVD and thousands of these have been distributed at church events and sporting fixtures all across the UK. People are constantly in touch with Stuart to say how this has been blessed in seeing someone saved in their district.

Looking out into the future, Stuart prays that God will lead him in his football and his ministry.

He has been 'capped' 37 times for his country and hopes to continue to be a blessing to the teams he represents at club and international level, both on and off the pitch, for as long as he is able to play.

His prime desire, though, is to serve God in evangelistic outreach.

Seeing men and women with all kinds of problems totally transformed in Christ. Seeing young people who had once been obsessed with sporting icons becoming passionate about Jesus.

Seeing others fired up with the burning desire he has to see their friends saved.

That's what it's all about.

Sporting trophies in lighted cabinets lose their sparkle after a while.

Stuart has his eye on something more permanent.

It is a crown of life, which is part of an eternal inheritance that will never spoil, perish or fade.

And he is thrilled for the Bible tells him that it is reserved in heaven, just for him.

What could be better than that?

*Other books by the same author*

———•••———

MY FATHER'S HAND
THIS IS FOR REAL
JUST THE WAY I AM
SOME PARTY IN HEAVEN
FIRST CITIZEN SMYTH
SOMETHING WORTH LIVING FOR
HOW SWEET THE SOUND
AS OUR HEADS ARE BOWED
ONLY THE BEST WILL DO
A BRUISED REED
BACK FROM THE BRINK
OUT OF THE MAZE
THE TANGLED LAMB
SOLDIER, SAILOR, LIVE OR DIE
I BELIEVE GOD
PAINTING THE TOWN RED
WHO CARES?
SIGN OF THE FISH
OUT OF THE DEEP
NOT BY MIGHT
A LITTLE CHILD SHALL LEAD THEM
AS WHITE AS SNOW
ROUGH DIAMONDS

———•••———

Contact Ambassador Productions +44 (0) 28 9045 0010
for your nearest stockist

**www.ambassador-productions.com**

**Dr. Noel Davidson** is a retired headmaster who has, within the last decade, become a popular and prolific author. He has developed his own distinctive style, which is a unique blend of authority and simplicity.
**Going For It!** is is twenty-fourth book.